The American Revolution and America's Role in the World

This book is the sixth in a series in AEI's
"We Hold These Truths: America at 250" initiative.

WE HOLD THESE TRUTHS: AMERICA AT 250

Democracy and the American Revolution

Capitalism and the American Revolution

Religion and the American Revolution

Natural Rights, the Common Good,
and the American Revolution

Slavery, Equality, and the American Revolution

The American Revolution and America's Role in the World

WE HOLD THESE TRUTHS

★ ★ ★ ★

AMERICA AT
— 250 —

The American Revolution and America's Role in the World

Edited by Yuval Levin,
Adam J. White, and John Yoo

AEI PRESS

Publisher for the American Enterprise Institute
WASHINGTON, DC

Library of Congress Cataloging-in-Publication Data

Names: Levin, Yuval editor | White, Adam J. editor | Yoo, John editor

Title: The American revolution and America's role in the world / edited by Yuval Levin, Adam J. White, John Yoo.

Description: Washington, DC : AEI Press, publisher for the American Enterprise Institute, [2025] | Series: We hold these truths : America at 250 ; 6 | Includes bibliographical references. | Summary: "The year 2026 marks the 250th anniversary of American independence, yet the founding is controversial now in ways it has not been in decades. The American Enterprise Institute offers a major intellectual and educational project to reintroduce Americans to the unique value of their national inheritance. In the sixth volume of this series, scholars of American history and international relations survey how the United States defined its place among the community of nations following independence. As they noted in the Declaration, the revolutionaries understood that the success of their movement depended on "a decent respect to the opinions of mankind" and assistance from allies abroad. At the same time, disputes over foreign entanglements and neutrality fiercely divided Americans in the early republic. Looking at the founding-era debates over America's "empire of liberty" can inform the foreign policy questions we face today" —Provided by publisher.

Identifiers: LCCN 2025054043 (print) | LCCN 2025054044 (ebook) | ISBN 9780844751092 paperback | ISBN 9780844751108 epub

Subjects: LCSH: United States—Foreign relations—1775-1783 | United States—History—Revolution, 1775-1783

Classification: LCC E249 .A545 2025 (print) | LCC E249 (ebook) | DDC 973.3—dc23/eng/20260212

LC record available at https://lccn.loc.gov/2025054043

LC ebook record available at https://lccn.loc.gov/2025054044

AEI PRESS

Publisher for the American Enterprise Institute for Public Policy Research
1789 Massachusetts Ave. NW, Washington, DC 20036
www.aei.org

Printed in the United States of America

Contents

Introduction

YUVAL LEVIN

July 4, 2026, will mark the 250th anniversary of the Declaration of Independence and, therefore, of the United States of America. In celebrating that milestone, Americans will naturally incline to highlight what is distinct about us and what separates us from other nations of the world. And yet the American founding cannot be understood apart from the international context in which it occurred and the international order that it transformed.

The founders were keenly aware that the world was watching them. The very first sentence of the Declaration of Independence sets the scene in global terms:

> When in the Course of human events, it becomes necessary for one people to dissolve the political bands which have connected them with another, and to assume among the powers of the earth, the separate and equal station to which the Laws of Nature and of Nature's God entitle them, a decent respect to the opinions of mankind requires that they should declare the causes which impel them to the separation.

The case the Declaration makes for revolution then rests on a set of grievances that are presented as facts to be submitted "to a candid world." And in the end, the Declaration asserts that the goal of the American Revolution is to establish

that these United Colonies are, and of Right ought to be Free
and Independent States; that they are Absolved from all Allegiance to the British Crown, and that all political connection
between them and the State of Great Britain, is and ought to
be totally dissolved; and that as Free and Independent States,
they have full Power to levy War, conclude Peace, contract
Alliances, establish Commerce, and to do all other Acts and
Things which Independent States may of right do.

That founding generation of Americans, in other words, fought to
establish America's place among the nations. And they knew that they
could succeed only if they played their part in the great game of the
European powers. The founding also established some basic patterns of
American foreign policy that endured for many decades and that, in some
respects, continue even now to shape our country's sense of its place in
global politics. It is not possible to understand our country, its history,
and its character without a sense of how the Revolution became an event
of international significance.

Better understanding our country is precisely the purpose of the American Enterprise Institute's "We Hold These Truths: America at 250" initiative, an ambitious celebration of the founding of which this volume forms
a part. Over several years leading up to the anniversary of the Declaration of Independence, we are inviting scholars both within AEI and from
other institutions to take up a series of themes important to understanding the American Revolution. These scholars represent a variety of fields
and viewpoints, so they will approach each of these themes from various
angles. The papers they produce will be published in a series of edited
volumes intended to help Americans think more deeply and clearly about
our nation's origins, character, and prospects.

The American Revolution and America's Role in the World is the sixth of
those books. Its chapters began as papers presented at an AEI conference held at the George Washington Presidential Library at Mount Vernon on April 24, 2025. Other volumes in the series consider the American

Revolution in relation to other themes, such as democracy, religion, natural rights, and the Constitution. In each case, our goal is to help reintroduce readers to their nation's history, thereby enabling them to maturely appreciate the reasons for celebrating the extraordinary milestone of its 250th anniversary.

In the chapters that follow, six eminent scholars of history, law, and government consider how we ought to understand the American Revolution as a global event and how it changed the international order.

William Anthony Hay examines some of the global precedents that inspired the Revolution and its leaders. He considers what was new and unique about the founding and what was an extension of deep and ingrained patterns of European politics.

Jeremy Rabkin traces the commitment of the founding generation to the law of nations and how the founders understood the rules of the international order in relation to the principles that shaped American political thought.

Gary J. Schmitt highlights the principles of statesmanship implicit in the Declaration of Independence and shows how different generations of American leaders adopted and adapted these as the United States gradually evolved into a global superpower.

Lindsay M. Chervinsky illuminates how international questions shaped the American independence movement and the politics of the early republic and traces the origins of American foreign policy.

Eliga H. Gould considers why America's first generation of statesmen sought to keep the new nation out of Europe's wars and how these efforts shaped two centuries and more of American diplomacy.

Walter Russell Mead shows just how central foreign policy concerns were to the architects of the American constitutional system and what lessons their thought might offer to leaders struggling to shape a 21st-century foreign policy for our country.

All of these arguments suggest that the United States has never been an insular or isolation-minded nation. From its earliest days, our society has understood that its prospects in a dangerous world depended on responsibly playing its part in global affairs—and assuming its separate and equal station among the powers of the earth.

1

The Revolution and Its Precedents

WILLIAM ANTHONY HAY

The Declaration of Independence's forthcoming 250th anniversary highlights the American Revolution as a transformative event while pointing to questions about America's role in the world. Walter McDougall evocatively contrasted the United States' role as a promised land set apart from old-world quarrels for more than a century after its founding with its later transformation into a crusader state imposing its vision around the globe. His framing in the 1990s stood at odds with triumphalist descriptions of the unipolar moment that followed the Cold War, but it tapped concerns that came to shape an increasingly contentious debate over the next quarter century.[1]

Those arguments point to an important set of questions, but what the struggle for independence meant for the United States and the world emerges at least as clearly from exploring precedents—both older precedents used to justify or understand the American Revolution and new ones set by the conflict. Upholding the claim to independence staked in 1776 shook the kaleidoscope of European politics to lasting effect by establishing the first new state since the Dutch Republic in the 1580s. Observers then had to discern the new picture and where they fit into it. Unspoken assumptions revealed by precedents indicated the thinking behind that process.

When Britain recognized American independence with the 1783 Treaty of Paris, Edmund Burke noted how "the appearance of a new state, of a new species, in a new part of the globe . . . has made as great a change in all the relations, and balances, and gravitation of power, as the appearance of a new planet would in the system of the solar world."[2] The image appealed to mechanistic assumptions in 18th-century thought while emphasizing the challenge of adapting to a different situation—as the new element American independence had added to the mix of European politics had upset a political balance already in flux.

Arguments made in the Declaration of Independence and by the example of successful revolt gave other peoples from the 1780s a ready template for their own circumstances.[3] Commentators linked the clash between Britain and its colonists with larger debates on liberty and governance. French leaders seeking revenge against Britain and recovery of their own position overseas expected that prolonged fighting would leave both sides exhausted, to France's own benefit. Intervention brought the French instead a crippling deficit that paralyzed governance within a decade, bringing on a revolution there and an independent American republic that severed ties with France in the 1790s. The United States exerted its own pull abroad even while struggling to resist foreign pressure during its turbulent early decades.[4]

Debates over politics and governance responded to events just as political action looked to the ideas those debates had aired for guidance or justification. Precedent conferred legitimacy on actions while giving contemporaries struggling to understand new changes a map to follow.

Lessons of the Dutch Revolt

The Dutch Revolt against Spain in the late 16th century, which established the Dutch Republic as a sovereign, independent state, provided the most obvious comparison for American independence. From the Stamp Act onward, the British and colonists alike drew a parallel with the clash between Philip II and his Dutch subjects as a cautionary tale on mishandling disputes. The Dutch Stadtholder William V, a cousin of the British king, saw the Declaration of Independence as a parody of the 1581 Act of Abjuration that repudiated allegiance to Spain. So did Hendrik Fagel, the secretary to the States General, who found comparing the actions of George III to Philip II's tyranny unreasonable. John Adams and other Americans, however, appealed to a community of experience with the Dutch. In both cases, the struggle for self-government became a war of national independence against a powerful empire aided by foreign intervention. Britons, Americans, and foreign observers looked to the earlier conflict as a guide.[5]

And there was much to learn from that precedent. Attempts to tighten royal control at the expense of customary local privileges and raise taxes against resistance by representative bodies drove the Netherlands to revolt in 1565. As a collection of provinces only recently welded into a political unit, the Low Countries had a tradition of rebelling in defense of their liberties that restricted arbitrary power. Their elites and population viewed allegiance as contingent on respect for their privileges and good governance. Costs from recent wars demanded revenue they resisted providing. Philip II's determination to impose religious orthodoxy by stamping out Protestantism reinforced an authoritarian turn backed by military force. Armed resistance brought a series of revolts that led to a civil war backed by English and French intervention, which then drew the conflict into a wider struggle across Western Europe.[6] The States General of the Netherlands formally repudiated their allegiance—and the king's authority—on July 26, 1581, in an Act of Abjuration that outlined the duties of princes to their subjects.

Not created by God for their rulers to submit and serve as slaves, subjects had claims of their own. The edict invoked positive and natural law to define a ruler who "deprive[s] them of their ancient liberty, privileges and customs" as a tyrant to be renounced and replaced before recounting actions that justified the break. "Despairing of all means of reconciliation and left without any other remedies and help," the Dutch abandoned Philip II "to pursue such means as we think likely to secure our rights, privileges and liberties."[7]

Even this cursory overview shows why Americans, notably Adams and Benjamin Franklin, compared their own struggle to that of the Netherlands. The South Carolina patriot William Henry Drayton spoke in 1776 of forcing George III to treat with the United States "as a free and independent people," just as the Dutch had made Philip II, whom he called "the most powerful prince in the old world," yield.[8] The Treaty of Antwerp in 1609 recognized the seven provinces as an independent Dutch Republic, and the Treaty of Münster formalized those terms in 1648. Two years later, an English writer, Owen Feltham, pointed to that struggle as the moment that checked Spain's ascendancy and began its decline.[9] The Dutch Revolt produced a flood of books in English, French, and Spanish, along with Latin volumes, engaging a transnational debate among men of letters. Prominent humanists, including the French historian Jacques Auguste de Thou, who lived through the struggle; the jurist Samuel von Pufendorf; and the English diplomat Sir William Temple were among those authors, along with Voltaire and Montesquieu, who took up the story generations later. Americans with a humanistic education or legal training, including Thomas Jefferson and others among the founders, would have read their works or been familiar with the arguments.[10]

Debates around the Dutch Revolt engaged questions about rights of resistance and foreign intervention in civil strife. Hugo Grotius, who wrote a history of the conflict in its shadow, limited the right of resistance to extreme circumstances because a promiscuous right threatened anarchy, "A Mob where all are speakers, and no Hearers."[11] Quoting Cicero that "any Peace is preferable to Civil War," he tapped 16th-century fears of divided authority and unrest that Thomas Hobbes and others also expressed. Grotius allowed resistance in which a ruler violated an established constitution either by abdicating, designing the destruction of his realm's people, or usurping a share of sovereignty held by a senate or people in a mixed regime. Even then, prudential action had to account for disturbance to the state and the destruction of innocents.[12] A century later, Emer de Vattel, an influential Swiss jurist, agreed that resisting a tyrant making war on the nation became self-defense but insisted that such defiance required intolerable evils and the long denial of justice to a people whose patience had been exhausted. He also distinguished rebellion from civil war between balanced parties, with the latter allowing foreign states to mediate or even aid the party they deemed to have the better cause.[13] The right to intervene under international law he asserted in 1758 would justify France and other countries in later supporting the United States against Britain.[14]

Precedents at Home

Other 17th-century precedents shaped responses to the American struggle for independence. Portugal's successful break from Spain in 1640 offered a weaker parallel; it had been independent as a separate monarchy with a distinct identity before Philip II took its crown in 1680 as the closest heir after its king died. But just as in America, foreign assistance played a critical role in that struggle, with the Dutch, English, and French intervening to reduce Spanish power for their own ends.[15] Upheavals within Britain during the 17th century—both the civil wars of the 1640s and the Glorious Revolution in 1688—that occurred in the shadow of nearby events in the Netherlands provided a reference point for comparison. Colonists and British alike saw the American Revolution through memories of the English Civil War, with New Englanders using rhetoric against Charles I to justify their own struggle.[16] Congress also took several grievances against George III from the Declaration of Rights that the Convention Parliament in 1689 issued to publicly justify deposing James II. Indeed, Charles James Fox, a British sympathizer to the colonists, thought Americans in the Declaration of Independence "had done no more than the English had done against James II."[17]

What the historian Hugh Trevor-Roper described as the general crisis of the 17th century fueled important debates over sovereignty, liberty, and political order amid the breakdown of governing systems in Europe that failed to adapt under strain.[18] Writing by Hobbes, James Harrington, and John Locke in the shadow of civil war in the British Isles and Continental unrest had lasting influence on political thought. A Commonwealth tradition among men who called themselves real or true Whigs kept alive principles of toleration, popular consent, and checks on executive power from the mid-century interregnum.[19] Their arguments resonated more in 18th-century America than in Britain, where upholding the political settlement following 1688 that established parliamentary supremacy and then the Hanoverian succession after 1714 made claims to a right of resistance suspect at best.

Indeed, competing precedents drew colonists and the metropole apart. British consensus accepted that the balanced constitution resting sovereignty with the King-in-Parliament joined principles of monarchy, aristocracy, and democracy in a dynamic equilibrium that secured liberty and property. Court Whigs thought it repudiated Stuart tyranny and the anarchy the interregnum had unleashed. Balance checked usurpation, whether by royal tyranny, aristocratic faction, or the people themselves. William Blackstone, Jean Louis de Lolme, and William Paley made mixed government canonical in their successive writings.[20] Even aside from the clash over imperial reform in the 1760s, the American preoccupation with older controversies from the previous century that their British counterparts thought had been settled created an important conceptual gap.[21]

The revival of intense Anglo-French rivalry in the 1740s that lasted until Napoleon's defeat at Waterloo in 1815 also shaped America's path to revolution, with the Seven Years' War a key episode.[22] Both in scope and its lasting effects, that conflict became the British Empire's first "great war." A vast program of naval mobilization and subsidies for European allies and colonists won sweeping gains that left Britain's rulers "captivated by but also adrift and at odds in a vast empire abroad and a new political world at home."[23]

What seemed a shared triumph for Britain and its colonies brought strife as bills for its stupendous cost came due. Fifty years of "salutary neglect" intended to avoid contention that might cause wider disruption had already ended. Deploying an army to check the French on the Ohio and then seize Canada exposed tensions even as Britain posted significant troops among colonists for the first time. Schemes to raise taxes and tighten metropolitan control emerged from the experience of military commanders and officials. Postwar expectations across the Atlantic diverged sharply from those of colonists anticipating a more secure and equal partnership within the empire and ministers determined to make regulation effective using parliamentary authority. That gap in perspective made disagreements harder to resolve, and removing a threat from France left colonists freer to challenge metropolitan authority.[24]

Winning the struggle for mastery in North America and securing maritime supremacy during the Seven Years' War brought other precedents to the fore. The balance of power, a concept that long shaped diplomatic thinking, reached beyond Europe to encompass maritime trade and colonies. Mercantilist theories influenced jurists who shaped international law. Partition treaties in 1698 and 1700 recognized the principle of a colonial balance of power, and the potential union of French and Spanish domains prompted the 1701–14 War of the Spanish Succession.

Britain, however, upset the overseas balance mid-century with strictly enforced blockades even before taking colonies from its foes.[25] Its admiralty courts in 1756 made enemy goods carried by nonbelligerents subject to capture. Neutrals denied a trade in peace could not conduct it during wartime as a temporary expedient for evading blockade. Besides keeping the Dutch from supplying French colonies, the "rule of 1756" punished them for neutrality. What the British deemed their maritime rights to impose strict blockades became a grievance to states that relied on free navigation.[26] Grotius's argument in *The Free Sea* (1609) that no monopoly could be established on the seas rightly open to the use of all nations and replies by English jurists claiming sovereignty in home waters provided important legal context for the later dispute.[27] Usurping maritime commerce enhanced Britain's wealth at the expense of other powers while making France and Spain second-rate powers, as Louis XV's foreign minister, the Duc de Choiseul, had presciently warned in 1758. That dynamic, he argued, was sufficient cause to unite Europe in curbing its ambitions.[28] British gains at the peace created an undercurrent felt over subsequent decades.

Diplomatic changes in Europe that left Britain isolated were less obvious than domestic and imperial challenges, but they would shape its problems in America. Concerns about cost had pushed ministers to seek peace rather than press for additional gains, but sharply ending the war and the subsidies it provided to stem its cost alienated an abandoned Prussia. Near defeat curbed Frederick II's aggression, turning a successful poacher who had extended his realm at Austrian expense into a more cautious gamekeeper with a stake in preserving his gains along with the status quo in Central Europe.[29]

Peace left France defeated and weakened, Prussia and Austria worn out, and Russia secure in the east and north. Competitive spheres diverged over the 1760s, with Eastern Europe disengaged from Western powers and Britain diplomatically isolated. Anglo-French rivalry overseas mattered less for Continental powers than their own interests beyond the Rhine, where Britain had little to offer.[30] Informed observers in London recognized the danger of lacking allies. Charles Jenkinson, a treasury official and member of Parliament, presciently warned in 1767, "We shall begin the next war with two enemies at a time," facing France and Spain with the Dutch neutral at best. Other European states jealous of Britain's commercial position would then strive to profit from the struggle.[31]

Unrest in America facilitated France's revenge and defense of the equilibrium Britain had disrupted. Choiseul sent agents to report on American sentiment from 1764, while Charles Gravier de Vergennes, who followed him in 1774, developed plans to secure France from conflict in Europe while allying with Spain.[32] Recovery from defeat took a decade, in which Versailles drew back on several occasions. Choiseul's immediate successor, the Duc d'Aiguillon, made an overture for cooperation the British rejected in 1773, turning the French back to cautious hostility with Vergennes appointed in his place. Tension in America dented British prestige. George III's remark in 1774 that "we must get the colonies into order before we engage with our neighbors" captured the situation, while a warning the next year by Sir Joseph York, ambassador to the Dutch Republic, that losing the colonies would make Britain "the scorn of Europe" expressed a growing concern about Britain's reputation. France, with its European borders largely secure, had a favorable position to strike a blow by the mid-1770s.[33]

A Transformed Global Order

The outbreak of the American Revolution is an oft-told story, but its swift and profound transformation of European international relations remains underappreciated. It broke long-standing precedents of European affairs and created a new and unfamiliar order.

The degree of sudden change was a function in part of persistent uncertainty about the precise nature of the American conflict with England. As noted, the Revolution's development as a constitutional dispute over liberties and local self-government highlighted parallels with the Dutch Revolt that contemporaries recognized.[34] And composite monarchies in which separate realms or states shared a single ruler were a recognizable framework to interpret the conflict.[35] Americans saw their relation to the British Crown in those terms. Franklin repeatedly distinguished the Crown's sovereignty over those possessions from that of the legislature, and he complained in 1767 that "every man in England seems to consider himself as a piece of a sovereign over America."[36]

Colonial appeals to George III for protection against ministers and Parliament clashed with how the British, including the king, who described himself revealingly as fighting the battle of the legislature, understood their constitution, under which unitary sovereignty rested with the King-in-Parliament.[37] Compromise became hard, especially after the Boston Tea Party brought coercive measures colonists resisted. British ministers saw the Declaration of Rights and Grievances by the Continental Congress in October 1774, with its accompanying trade boycott, as a move to intimidate them into concessions. What seemingly began over tea, as a German observer remarked in 1778, became a dispute over kingdoms.[38]

Congress acted as an effective national government after the clashes at Lexington and Concord, with British authority collapsing as rapidly across the other 13 colonies as in New England. Local communities filled the gap, managing their own affairs in a contingent, open-ended process that transformed American politics.[39] The royal proclamation on August 23, 1775, declaring the colonies in revolt effectively announced war, but rather than suppressing rebellion, British forces now had to defeat and displace an enemy regime.[40] Congress issued a series of state papers, including one on July 6, 1775, that justified taking up arms, presenting the case that culminated in the Declaration of Independence. Franklin noted how Vattel's work had been continually in their hands, with the jurist's arguments guiding congressional resolutions and policy. Adams and Richard Henry Lee recognized that securing foreign aid required formal separation from Britain so American representatives could have the status regular trade demanded.

The increasing need for supplies made recognition a pressing concern that Congress addressed through official documents, including model treaties, to enact independence through agreements of trade and alliance.[41] But despite Vattel's recent case for outside powers taking sides in civil war, established rules for neutral trade assumed war between independent states rather than groups within them. It remained unclear whether Americans fit that category or were merely exceptionally successful rebels until France recognized the United States in 1778. French action gave cover for de facto, if not de jure, recognition by other states.[42]

Sustaining resistance had made Congress look beyond American shores for support. Adams saw independence as the essential precondition for relations with other states that might provide aid once fighting had begun. Established trading networks through the Netherlands and Spain provided military supplies, even though the colonial economy was hampered by a lack of specie. Covert French and later Spanish aid funded American purchases, and both governments allowed the use of their ports. Vergennes remained cautious into 1776, and transferring supplies through a private company afforded plausible deniability.[43] A confrontation in South America with Portugal, a long-standing British ally, preoccupied Madrid until 1777.

Hopes to restore Britain's prestige in Europe by a quick victory prompted Lord George Germain, who directed the war in America as colonial secretary, to send an unprecedented force over the Atlantic in 1776. Concerns about alarming France or Spain kept Britain from fully mobilizing its navy to blockade colonies and support its army's operations. Besides practical difficulties covering such an extended coastline, an effective blockade would have also risked conflict with foreign governments that ministers sought to avoid. Needing peace in Europe to settle the American revolt, they also feared that weakness might embolden rivals there.[44]

Catherine II gave an early sign this resistance was a possibility by refusing a British request to hire 20,000 Russian troops for service in America. In contrast, Hanover, George III's other realm, had already provided five regiments for Gibraltar that freed British regulars. Bringing Russian troops into British pay had been considered in earlier wars for European service, and it fit the long-established *Soldatenhandel*, whereby German princes leased soldiers and regiments, but Catherine II rejected out of hand an offer she viewed as treating her empire as a minor principality and her as "a glorified *Landgräfin*" rather than ruler of a great power. The tsarina's adviser Nikita Panin noted that a colonial revolt might set a dangerous example but stressed the prospect of trade opportunities and curbing British dominance at sea.[45] Officials in London turned instead to Germany, where Hesse-Cassel and Brunswick had offered regiments. Known as Hessians (after the region most of them came from), those nearly 30,000 trained and disciplined men proved critical to British efforts.[46] But the minor states providing those troops marked the exception to the British diplomatic isolation that tightened from 1778.

The American struggle for independence never followed a linear path. Advantage shifted back and forth, with the outcome uncertain before the final months.[47] Britain recovered from the forced withdrawal of its army from Boston in 1776 to capture New York and New Jersey, driving George Washington's Continental Army over the Delaware River. Resistance seemed near collapse, as Samuel Adams and Washington both remarked.[48] Defeats at Trenton and Princeton, however, knocked the British back, with Saratoga later a humiliating loss. French intervention forced the British to abandon captured Philadelphia and concentrate at New York in 1778, where Charles d'Estaing's fleet temporarily isolated them. British troops under Sir Henry Clinton later recovered the initiative to mount successful campaigns in Georgia and the Carolinas by capturing Charleston in 1780, a defeat for the United States comparable to Saratoga. British ministers thought another successful campaign would force the French to make terms, and Washington lamented in April 1781 "that we are at the end of our tether, and that now or never our deliverance must come."[49] Yorktown resolved Washington's fears, but it was an awfully near-run thing.

John Burgoyne's surrender at Saratoga opened the way for French intervention, though Vergennes also feared that Americans risked defeat without direct support. Their independence, he recognized early, would redress the imbalance of power by throwing considerable weight behind France or some other state while denying Britain the advantages of controlling them.[50] French preparations for hostilities, including a long-term naval mobilization project, were ready in early 1778, as diplomats settled terms for an alliance stipulating that neither party would make peace without American independence.

The alliance committing France to join the war offered more than the commercial treaty Congress had sought. Formally announcing the commissioners in a presentation before Louis XVI on March 20, 1778, marked the first official reference to the United States as a sovereign, independent state. Spain held back from such recognition and for a time suspended its financial assistance, but New Orleans, which it controlled, remained a supply route through the Mississippi.[51] Careful French diplomacy avoided repeating the division of effort between Europe and overseas colonies that had produced defeat in both during the Seven Years' War. It kept in check tensions over a disputed succession in Bavaria and between Russia and the Ottomans that might have started a larger war. The cool responses that British overtures drew from Austria, Prussia, and Russia helped Vergennes's efforts to shape a favorable environment as tensions with Britain grew before the open break.[52]

The expanded global war in 1778 forced Britain to shift resources from North America to keep hold of vital interests in the Caribbean and change its overall strategy. Efforts to regain the mainland colonies gave way to a strategic defensive combined with opportunistic attacks exploiting local vulnerabilities to keep Washington on guard.[53] Fighting would also extend beyond the Western Hemisphere to European waters—Gibraltar and the Channel Islands both faced attacks—and India, but not Europe, where peace defended France's landward flank. With Americans treated as legitimate belligerents rather than rebels from the start, the conflict already had turned, as Sir George Savile remarked, "by degrees from a question of right and wrong between subjects, to a war between us and a foreign nation."[54] The alliance with France hardened that tendency. Spain joined the war as an ally of France—though not formally of the United States—in 1779, after failed mediation overtures to Britain. The collapse of Anglo-Dutch relations over trade with America and carrying cargoes for belligerent powers then added a traditional ally to Britain's growing list of foes in late 1780.

Disputes over neutral rights became an important factor as Britain asserted a legal claim to impose strict blockades that other states resisted. While circumstances during the Seven Years' War had favored that insistence, diplomatic isolation now created a different situation, which France exploited. Halting trade in naval stores—timber, hemp or rope, and other items used to maintain ships—between countries on the Baltic and France and Spain sparked clashes that brought the Dutch into the war and promoted a league of armed neutrality that complicated British efforts.[55] Because seizures affected trade beyond consignments for America, Austria's Joseph II called such "despotism at sea" an "incredible and intolerable" burden.[56]

While Denmark, Sweden, and Prussia protested the seizure of their ships, the former two governments had weakened their case by conceding the expansive British definition of contraband in past treaties. The Danish foreign minister, however, sketched principles for liberal trade that Russia would later propose formally.[57] Catherine II's Declaration of Armed Neutrality in 1780 stipulated free navigation between ports for nonbelligerent ships, protections for persons and their effects outside recognized contraband, and enforcement close to shore for a blockade to be legally effective. While Russia had long supported liberal rules for wartime trade at sea, the issue largely helped raise the tsarina's prestige by defending neutral maritime states. It caught Britain off guard, especially when France and Spain accepted Russian terms, even as a bluff Catherine never intended to uphold by force. Sweden and Denmark acceded to the league, with Austria, Portugal, and Prussia signing the next year and Naples in 1783.[58] Frederick II looked to profit from whatever opportunities the American war offered while reflecting on whether British power had peaked and begun to decline.[59]

Mediation offers implicitly recognized a new status for the United States, if not the sovereign independence Americans claimed. Spain had already offered its own before joining the war and suggested its 1609 armistice with the Dutch as a precedent. Austria proposed mediation in 1779, with Russia later joining the overture. While they approached Britain, France, and Spain rather than Congress, Russian plans envisioned American representation at a conference in Leipzig to discuss terms and implicitly expected them to decide their own fate. The Russo-Austrian proposal in May 1781 for a general negotiation at Vienna invited Americans who would settle a separate peace with Britain unless either party requested mediation. Financial strain on France made Vergennes willing to consider discussions, but France's commitment to American independence made settling on acceptable terms unlikely.[60] Open to an accommodation with the French and Spanish, British ministers refused to negotiate with Americans, and George III rejected interference by any foreign state "in the terms for bringing my rebellious subjects to a sense of their crimes." Ironically, such intransigence favored the United States after Yorktown by preventing a less favorable earlier compromise based on territory held by each side before then.[61]

While Germain and George III wanted to persevere, they had neither the military force nor the political support to do so. Lord Frederick North, the prime minister, took the news of Yorktown like a gunshot to the body and declared it all over.[62] A new British administration would try to divide the enemy alliance by offering Americans concessions to induce a separate peace. Fighting beyond America continued with British naval victories in the Caribbean evening the balance with France. Spain's inability to capture Gibraltar forced Madrid to lower its terms as its French ally felt increasing financial strain. Lord Shelburne, who replaced Germain as colonial secretary and later became prime minister, directed American negotiations, which followed a separate track from those with France treating for Spain and the Dutch, and he hoped at first to keep the 13 colonies in a loose relationship with Britain. He soon yielded to reality in conceding political independence while aiming to preserve effective rather than de jure control by economically dominating the United States as its primary trading partner and financier.

A position that followed earlier assessments during the struggle would guide subsequent British policy toward the United States. Shelburne offered generous frontiers up to the Mississippi River, though he refused Franklin's demand for Canada. The agreement settling terms with America on November 30, 1782, would not take effect until France and Britain also settled the next year. A final treaty signed in Paris on September 3, 1783, specifically acknowledged the former colonies "to be free sovereign and independent states."[63]

Precedents for Revolts and Revolutions

British recognition in 1783 secured de jure standing for the United States' de facto independence, making the Treaty of Paris one of the country's founding documents. It highlights the relational side of independence, with its validity resting on formal acceptance. Rights had to be acknowledged for them to carry weight. Americans sought to uphold their standing with other states while strictly defending the symbols and substance of sovereignty. Hence the persistent insistence on reciprocal treatment by foreign governments.[64] Eighteenth-century jurists, as David Armitage notes, had not resolved the question of how, when, and under what terms states might acquire the rights of sovereignty and equal standing that Vattel argued natural law provided. Third-party recognition for many authorities did not suffice and lacked constructive force until the former sovereign renounced its rights.

A party refusing obedience might effectively come to possess the independence it demanded and thereby turn the dispute into one between independent states, but the sovereign could construe aid from an outside party as an act of war. Americans had forced the question of recognition to create a new precedent, with the Treaty of Paris confirming the change much as Spanish recognition had done earlier for the Dutch. European jurists accordingly incorporated the Declaration of Independence and other American documents into the positive law of nations as precedents alongside earlier international treaties.[65]

Ideological concerns about republicanism in the United States mattered less for other countries than practical considerations around trade and neutral rights at sea that shaped their actions. One Venetian account saw "the rebellion of the Anglo-Americans" at the point of forming ideas "capable of subverting all nations," but another Italian found the colonists' will to preserve liberties menaced by reform legitimate and natural. Tuscany's Hapsburg Grand Duke Leopold, who would succeed his brother Joseph II as Austria's ruler, took a sympathetic interest while corresponding with Jefferson's friend Filippo Mazzei and studying Pennsylvania's constitution as a guide to reform.[66]

Local preoccupations shaped the reception of American news transmitted through Paris or the Netherlands, whose culture then remained in the French orbit, often copied directly from British publications.[67] Spanish authorities feared the example it set for their own American empire, with the Count of Aranda warning in 1783 that the United States would eventually grow into a power eager to absorb Florida and Mexico. Revolts in Peru and La Plata, along with earlier protests in the 1760s, sharpened those concerns. Francisco de Miranda, a Venezuelan officer who fought at Pensacola and subsequently lived in the United States, saw its independence as "the infallible preliminary to our own."[68] Latin America's independence, however, came much later, from internal and European dynamics rather than influences from the United States.

The effects of independence over the next few years tested expectations. Britain lost the war for America, but France gained neither trade nor prestige to compensate for expenses that brought its public finances into crisis by the late 1780s.[69] Fear of decline had driven the British to persist against growing odds. George III saw the war in 1781 as a contest over "whether we are to rank among the Great Powers of Europe or be reduced to one of the most inconsiderable." Others echoed his alarm, fearing "imperial sway, national dignity, ostentation, and luxury must with our commerce be annihilated" on losing America. Joseph II, who thought it a product of British misrule, told his brother Leopold in 1783 that Britain was no longer a great power but instead a second-rank state, comparable to Sweden or Denmark.[70]

Recovery instead followed a clean political break with America. Adam Smith and Josiah Tucker had shown that the advantages of American trade to Britain did not rest on direct political control. Shelburne became the first of many British figures hoping to dominate the United States economically as its best customer and primary supplier of finance and manufactured goods without the burden of governing or defending it. The conflict, like earlier wars, ceased to be a point of partisan dispute and passed into history.[71] William Pitt accepted the outcome without apologizing for the effort when he told Parliament in 1787 that "our resistance must be admired, and in our defeats we gave proofs of our greatness and almost-inexhaustible resources."[72] Those resources left Britain well positioned for the next crisis, which soon came.

The historian R. R. Palmer famously located American independence in an age of democratic revolutions between 1760 and 1800, but the period's instability was more apparent to contemporaries than was popular involvement with politics. Domestic and international tensions paralleled the general crisis of the preceding century. The instability's expressions within states took different forms, from Pugachev's Revolt in Russia and royal coups in Denmark and Sweden to the American crisis and a failure of institutional reform in France.[73] Diplomatic rules that set a premium on compensation for gains by others and indemnities for services to allies or a state's own losses destabilized Europe from the 1760s, making conflict more likely and the stakes far higher in what became a zero-sum game.[74]

Equilibrium faltered in the 1780s as foreign defeats upset domestic politics while internal disruption impeded protecting interests abroad. Losing a political struggle in the Netherlands to Britain became a catalyst for the French Revolution, and the ensuing distraction that removed France from international politics helped the British face down Spain over the Nootka Sound dispute in 1790 and gave Austria, Prussia, and Russia a free hand in their final partitions of Poland. Revolution swept aside restraints on mobilizing French resources behind aggressive moves beyond the country's borders. The war that began in 1792 would last more than two decades, until Napoleon's final defeat at Waterloo in 1815.

That protracted conflict reached over the Atlantic just as American examples influenced early stages of the French Revolution. Washington and Franklin had both become celebrities in fashionable circles, with the former embodying an increasingly popular type of civic virtue looking back to republican Rome. Exemplary men impressed Europeans more than documents French revolutionaries themselves seem not to have quoted.[75] A tradition-minded revolt against Joseph II's centralizing reforms in the Austrian Netherlands did take the Declaration of Independence in 1790 as a model for repudiating allegiance. It modified American precedent along with older forms of protest for their own purposes.[76]

French revolutionaries would soon reject the examples from America and Britain that some of them had originally embraced, while foreigners—including Americans like Gouverneur Morris and John Adams—rejected their project. Adams used Enrico Caterino Davila's 17th-century history of the French Wars of Religion as a precedent to frame the unfolding events in France with a 1790 pamphlet titled *Discourses on Davila*.[77] Friedrich von Gentz, a German admirer of Burke and later private secretary to the Austrian Chancellor Prince Klemens von Metternich, denied that the American Revolution followed the same principles as that of France in a pamphlet John Quincy Adams translated and published in 1800. It was, Gentz insisted, a defensive political change rather than an overturning of social and moral order. The federal Constitution of 1789 then secured orderly government under law.[78] France's unfolding revolution changed the context for understanding events across the Atlantic that observers with different views cited for their own arguments or purposes.

Precedents for American Foreign Policy

New precedents emerged from what American independence meant to other states amid a protracted global war and how the United States tried to uphold it. Lesser states had a recognized place within the international order as buffers separating interests of larger powers, which Burke's image of a new body in the solar system recognized. Their role, however, came under increasing pressure as they sought to avoid being swamped by currents they could not control. Distance did not spare the United States. Indeed, it struggled with problems other neutral powers had faced during the American war for independence.

Precedents from those years became a foundation for the country's approach to foreign relations. John Adams had insisted that neutrality in European wars was the basis of real, if not nominal, independence, as foreign states otherwise "would find means to corrupt our people, to influence our councils," making Americans "little better than puppets, danced on the wires of the cabinets of Europe."[79] French demands for support triggered a debate that divided Washington's cabinet and showed how foreign disputes could divide Americans. Along with Washington's later warning against "entangling alliances" in his Farewell Address, the neutrality proclamation sparked the Pacificus–Helvidius Debates in published letters between Alexander Hamilton and James Madison.[80] Conspiracies by James Wilkinson and, later, Aaron Burr highlighted vulnerabilities along with the government's limited means to control peripheral regions.[81]

Frequent trade and cultural ties, Secretary of State Edmund Randolph argued in 1794, brought the United States the same rights and privileges as other states despite the country's newly recognized sovereignty and geographic location "without the European circle."[82] Upholding those claims in practice, however, required force along with diplomacy. The United States fought the Quasi-War with France from 1798 to 1800, until a new French government headed by Napoleon conceded the principle of free navigation the United States demanded.[83] Attacks on American ships by Barbary States in North Africa led Jefferson to send a squadron to the Mediterranean. Defending American neutrality and the freedom of navigation and trade shaped foreign policy as it became harder to avoid conflict.[84]

The French Revolutionary Wars ended in the early 1800s with fundamental differences unresolved and another round of conflict likely. Britain, which had purged the Orient of European rivals while defeating local powers, had secured a near monopoly of overseas trade, which cast it in the invidious position of decrying French ambitions as its own gains rose.[85] Gentz described jealousy of British power in 1800 as the dominant principle of Europe's political writers. Britain's wealth meant poverty for the Continent, while its industrial and commercial might were hateful monopolies.[86] Americans, as an envoy to London declared, believed the British prolonged Europe's agony for their own advantage by setting unreasonable peace terms.[87]

Even as he recognized the danger France posed until the Louisiana Purchase, Jefferson saw alignment with Britain during the 1790s as a strategic error that curbed American independence. He hoped Russia, which had sponsored a failed armed neutrality effort in 1800, might serve as a counterweight and defender of neutral rights.[88] Russian officials similarly looked to the United States as a counterweight to Britain, which not only ruled the waves but persistently waived the rules to its own advantage. Count Nikolai Rumiantsev, Alexander I's foreign minister, considered British control over his country's overseas trade an affront and a threat of "dominion something like they had in India." Priorities changed as French pressure on Russia grew, but the United States remained a factor in political calculations.[89]

Neutrality became untenable as the war revived in 1803 following a brief peace between Britain and France. Jefferson cited the Royal Navy's 1807 bombardment of Copenhagen to secure the Danish fleet alongside Napoleon's aggressions as proof of an epoch marked by "the total extinction of national morality."[90] British sea power locked French imperial ambitions into Europe, where other great powers resisted Napoleon's efforts to build a counterweight by dominating the Continent.[91] The United States could not avoid involvement without giving up its own trade. Jefferson's Embargo Act, in response to the rival belligerents' measures, provoked domestic opposition while perplexing the British as a self-defeating policy. Clashes with the Royal Navy, unresolved border issues, and ambitions to gain Canada led to an American declaration of war that made the United States effectively Napoleon's partner at a point when the larger conflict began turning against France.[92]

The War of 1812 was a second war for independence from Britain and a theater of the larger struggle that closed at Waterloo in 1815. Ending in a draw, in which both sides accepted the status quo ante bellum and the United States held New Orleans at the mouth of the Mississippi River, the conflict showed that Americans would fight for national honor and sovereignty, but it left them chastened by the experience. The danger of being drawn into European disputes underlined the importance of neutrality to preserving independence and the difficulty of maintaining it.[93] American leaders over the coming decades took the War of 1812 as an example of what to avoid by following the guidance of Adams and Washington.

Latin American independence soon put those principles to the test with the Monroe Doctrine in 1823, effectively separating Europe and the Americas to the United States' advantage. Differences stand out from Britain's earlier struggles with its colonists. Spanish officials contained revolts more effectively, and the character of the colonial societies they ruled neither allowed for popular participation in governance nor created an experienced political class that could lead. Rebellion operated typically as a negotiating position that triggered further bargaining rather than armed repression, and concessions to it did not compromise fundamental legitimacy.[94]

Crisis came only when Napoleon's occupation of Spain in 1808 created a power vacuum across an empire based on royal absolutism.[95] The postwar period restored monarchy, then struggled to impose rule on colonies where elites had seized power often to preserve order and their own position against chaos. Stability in ethnically divided societies proved elusive amid escalating violence. Washington and other founders of the United States, with Franklin a significant exception, had less experience with Europe than the liberators of Spanish America, but they had greater practical experience of governing than those later men and a political order adapted to republican principles. Such differences mattered. European ideas and the more immediate experience of the French Revolution cast a longer shadow over Latin America than precedents in the United States did.[96]

The Declaration of Independence stands out as an exception in providing a template for revolutionaries asserting claims. Haitians issued a declaration in January 1804 modeled on that of the United States, albeit directed to their own people rather than a candid world. Spanish declarations of founding documents circulated through Latin America. An Ecuadorian called the Declaration of Independence "the true political decalogue," though his counterparts looked for equality and home rule instead of independence and separation. Venezuela became the first to make that wider demand for independence in 1811, followed over the decade by Argentina, Chile, and other regions farther north.[97]

Latin America's revolutionaries, however, struggled to establish a viable political order that could sustain their claims by mobilizing resources and popular support to govern effectively. Madison captured their problem when he noted the difficulty of creating a government able to control the people and itself that could thereby avoid swinging between anarchy and tyranny. Countering ambition with ambition secured a balanced political order for the United States, but the achievement rested on institutions and practices from Britain that Americans kept when they claimed independence, along with traditions of local self-government. Having largely inherited a system of political organization, they did not have to create one, but those conditions did not provide a template to apply in very different circumstances.[98]

Spain's inability to enforce its authority over the colonies in revolt created the conditions by 1815 that Vattel had argued would justify recognition. Foreign governments, including the United States, accordingly faced a decision they sought to avoid. John Quincy Adams likened the situation in late 1817 to debates over the French Revolution, when "ardent spirits" would rush into the conflict without regard for consequences. He saw only troubles on all sides in a cauldron of unrest, "which will soon be at boiling heat."[99] Those troubles bolstered arguments from the 1790s for American neutrality, and the United States delayed recognition until the new republics showed they could sustain the independence they claimed. An 1820 revolution in Spain that began among soldiers destined for America, along with its parallel in Naples, threw European politics into disorder. French intervention backed by other powers to restore the Spanish king raised concerns about whether it would extend to the New World. European states lacked the capacity to aid Spain, whose efforts had already failed, but their opposition to revolution made recognition a symbolic issue for governments determined to contain unrest closer to home.[100]

Events leading to the Monroe Doctrine show how European states treated the United States as part of the international system and Americans' reluctance to restrict their own freedom of action. Britain granted the Latin American republics de facto recognition in 1821 to protect its trade and curb piracy while urging other powers to follow. It also sought backing from the United States to keep France from leveraging influence over Spain into a stronger position in the New World.[101] Hostile rhetoric by Continental European powers had raised fears that made James Monroe and several former presidents, including the Anglophobic Jefferson and Madison, open to cooperation. John Quincy Adams pushed instead for a unilateral declaration that would uphold neutrality while excluding new European involvement in the Western Hemisphere. Such a declaration also kept the United States out of European questions about which it lacked the means to act effectively. The Monroe Doctrine, along with accompanying but less noted diplomatic letters, made that point to lasting effect. It became a lasting principle in American foreign policy, albeit with more attention to excluding foreign influence in the New World than restraint toward the Old World.[102]

One and the Same System

The absence of general war in Europe between Napoleon's defeat at Waterloo and the outbreak of World War I favored American detachment. European conflicts over that near century tended to be limited in scope and duration, which contained their effects. The most devastating conflicts, including the American Civil War, occurred elsewhere. By contrast, protracted struggles during the 18th and 20th centuries, including the Cold War, made neutrality difficult.

Whether as colonial subjects of the British Crown or citizens of the United States, Americans found it hard to stand apart from general wars in Europe that became global conflicts. The long 19th-century peace, however, allowed the United States to grow and resolve its own disputes without foreign interference. Concerns about freedom of navigation and neutral rights faded from view without the conflicts that had made them pressing issues. Fears during the 1780s and 1790s of foreign domination never came to pass. Americans instead focused on their own country's development. The eventual transition from wealth to power in the late 19th century again transformed America's place in the international system that securing independence had provided.[103]

John Quincy Adams revealingly cited the first Treaty of Amity and Commerce with France in 1778 as a pivotal document. Its preamble was, he told the American minister to Colombia in 1823, to commercial relations with foreign governments what the Declaration of Independence was to internal government: "The two instruments were parts of one and the same system."[104] His words highlight the connection between the American Revolution and the United States' role in the world. Precedents that shaped them shed light on the story, as do the precedents established after independence over the early decades of the republic. They provided a guide for statesmen grappling with challenges in those years and a map for observers today looking back to understand one of the most pivotal moments in modern history.

Notes

1. Walter A. McDougall, *Promised Land, Crusader State: The American Encounter with the World Since 1776* (Houghton Mifflin, 1997); and Charles Krauthammer, "The Unipolar Moment," *Foreign Affairs* 70, no. 1 (1990–91): 23–33, https://users.metu.edu.tr/utuba/Krauthammer.pdf. Francis Fukuyama introduced the concept with an influential parallel take in Francis Fukuyama, *The End of History and the Last Man* (Free Press, 1992). Robert Kagan makes a case against McDougall's position in Robert Kagan, *Dangerous Nation: America's Place in the World from Its Earliest Days to the Dawn of the Twentieth Century* (Knopf, 2006).

2. *The Works and Correspondence of the Right Honorable Edmund Burke*, ed. Charles William et al., 2nd ed. (London, 1852), 2:453.

3. David Armitage, *The Declaration of Independence: A Global History* (Harvard University Press, 2007), 13–15.

4. Paul W. Schroeder, *The Transformation of European Politics 1763–1848* (Clarendon Press, 1994), 38–39.

5. G. C. Gibbs, "The Dutch Revolt and the American Revolution," in *Royal and Republican Sovereignty in Early Modern Europe: Essays in Memory of Ragnhild Hatton*, ed. Robert Oresko and G. C. Gibbs (Cambridge University Press, 1997).

6. There is a standard account in Geoffrey Parker, *The Dutch Revolt* (Cornell University Press, 1977).

7. E. H. Kossman and A. F. Mellink, eds., *Texts Concerning the Revolt of the Netherlands* (Cambridge University Press, 1974), 216–28.

8. Stephen E. Lucas, "The Plakkaat van Verlatinge: A Neglected Model for the American Declaration of Independence," in *Connecting Cultures: The Netherlands in Five Centuries of Transatlantic Exchange*, ed. Rosemarijn Hoefte and Johanna C. Kardux (VU University Press, 1994), 199–200.

9. Parker, *The Dutch Revolt*, 239–40, 265–66, 270. Feltham's point resonated in 18th-century Britain and the United States amid fear of losing power or political virtue. Ironically, the Dutch Republic's decline from great power to complacent prosperity became a cautionary tale for John Adams. See also Dennis C. Rasmussen, *Fears of a Setting Sun: The Disillusionment of America's Founders* (Princeton University Press, 2021).

10. Lucas, "The Plakkaat van Verlatinge," 200–2; and G. J. Schutte, "'A Subject of Admiration and Encomium': The History of the Dutch Republic as Interpreted by Non-Dutch Authors in the Second Half of the Eighteenth Century," in *Clio's Mirror: Historiography in Britain and the Netherlands*, ed. A. C. Duke and C. A. Tamse (De Walburg Press, 1985), 111–12, 116–17.

11. Hugo Grotius, *The Rights of War and Peace*, ed. Richard Tuck (Liberty Fund, 2005), 1:240, 338–39.

12. Grotius, *The Rights of War and Peace*, 1:258, 375–78, 381; and David Armitage, *Civil Wars: A History in Ideas* (Knopf, 2017), 105–8.

13. Emer de Vattel, *The Law of Nations* [. . .], ed. Bela Kaposi and Richard Whatmore (Liberty Fund, 2008), 425–26, 429–30.

14. Armitage, *Civil Wars*, 133–34.

15. J. H. Elliott, "The Spanish Monarchy and the Kingdom of Portugal, 1580–1640," in *Conquest and Coalescence: The Shaping of the State in Early Modern Europe*, ed. Mark Greengrass (Edward Arnold, 1991), 65.

16. J. C. D. Clark, *The Language of Liberty, 1660–1832: Political Discourse and Social Dynamics in the Anglo-American World* (Cambridge University Press, 1994), 266–67, 356–68.

17. Lucas, "The Plakkaat van Verlatinge," 191. Armitage notes that Vattel cited William III's 1688 expedition as a precedent for intervention. Armitage, *Civil Wars*, 133.

18. H. R. Trevor-Roper, "The General Crisis of the Seventeenth-Century," *Past & Present* 16 (November 1959): 31–64, https://www.jstor.org/stable/650152.

19. Caroline Robbins, *The Eighteenth-Century Commonwealthman: Studies in the Transmission, Development and Circumstances of English Liberal Thought from the Restoration of Charles II Until the War with the Thirteen Colonies* (Harvard University Press, 1959).

20. Reed Browning, *Political and Constitutional Ideas of the Court Whigs* (Louisiana State University Press, 1982), 196–97; H. T. Dickinson, *Liberty and Property: Political Ideology in Eighteenth-Century Britain* (Holmes and Meier, 1977), 143, 149–50; and Angus Hawkins, *Victorian Political Culture: "Habits of Heart and Mind"* (Oxford University Press, 2015), 34–35.

21. Clark, *The Language of Liberty, 1660–1832*, 9.

22. Hamish Scott describes the period to Napoleon's defeat in 1815 as the Seventy Years War, with intense peacetime rivalry punctuating open conflict. He argues that larger protracted struggle is important for understanding the American Revolution and its global impact. Hamish Scott, *The Birth of a Great Power System, 1740–1815* (Routledge, 2006), 74.

23. Lawrence Henry Gipson, "The American Revolution as an Aftermath of the Great War for the Empire, 1754–63," *Political Science Quarterly* 65, no. 1 (1950): 87, 89, https://www.psqonline.org/article.cfm?IDArticle=6095; and Linda Colley, *Britons: Forging the Nation, 1707–1837* (Yale University Press, 1992), 87–102.

24. Patrick Griffin, *America's Revolution* (Oxford University Press, 2012), 7–8, 30–35; and Jack P. Greene, "The Seven Years' War and the American Revolution: The Causal Relationship Reconsidered," in *The British Atlantic Empire Before the American Revolution*, ed. Peter Marshall and Glyn Williams (Routledge, 1980), 87–102.

25. Max Savelle, "The American Balance of Power and European Diplomacy, 1713–78," in *The Era of the American Revolution: Studies Inscribed to Evarts Boutell Greene*, ed. Richard B. Morris (Columbia University Press, 1939), 140–41, 158.

26. Matt Schumann and Karl W. Schweizer, *The Seven Years War: A Transatlantic History* (Routledge, 2008), 105; Julian S. Corbett, *England in the Seven Years War: A Study in Combined Strategy*, 2 vols. (Longmans, Green, 1907); Savelle, "The American Balance of Power and European Diplomacy, 1713–78," 160; and Charles Jenkinson, *A Discourse on the Conduct of the Government of Great-Britain in Respect to Neutral Nations During the Present War* (London, 1758).

27. Hugo Grotius, *The Free Sea*, ed. David Armitage (Liberty Fund, 2004). The English jurist John Selden challenged his claim in John Selden, *Mare Clausum* (London, 1635). Selden argued the sea could be appropriated for exclusive use as much as territory on land.

28. Savelle, "The American Balance of Power and European Diplomacy, 1713–78," 160–61.

29. Richard Middleton, *The Bells of Victory: The Pitt–Newcastle Ministry and the Conduct of the Seven Years' War, 1757–1762* (Cambridge University Press, 1985), 158–60; Andrew Roberts, *The Last King of America: The Misunderstood Reign of George III* (Viking, 2021), 93, 96, 101–3; and Tim Blanning, *Frederick the Great: King of Prussia* (Random House, 2016), 325–26.

30. Schroeder, *The Transformation of European Politics, 1763–1848*, 3–5; and H. M. Scott, *British Foreign Policy in the Age of the American Revolution* (Clarendon Press, 1990), 67, 85.

31. Andrew Roberts rightly defines "finding a stable ministry which had the confidence of both King and Parliament" as the decade's central problem. Roberts, *The Last King of America*, 109, 171; and Charles Jenkinson, "Heads of Defense of the Extra Estimate of the Navy," British Library Additional Manuscript 38336, 366–67.

32. Samuel Flagg Bemis, *The Diplomacy of the American Revolution* (Encounter Books, 2023), 13–15.

33. Jonathan R. Dull, *A Diplomatic History of the American Revolution* (Yale University Press, 1985), 36–39; and Scott, *British Foreign Policy in the Age of the American Revolution*, 194–95.

34. Jack P. Greene lays out this interpretation in Jack P. Greene, *The Constitutional Origins of the American Revolution* (Cambridge University Press, 2011).

35. J. H. Elliott, "A Europe of Composite Monarchies," *Past & Present*, no. 137 (November 1992): 48–71, https://www.jstor.org/stable/650851; and Jenny Wormald, "The Creation of Britain: Multiple Kingdoms or Core and Colonies?," *Transactions of the Royal Historical Society* 2 (1992): 175–94, https://www.jstor.org/stable/3679104.

36. Benjamin Franklin, "Marginalia in Protests of the Lords Against Repeal of the Stamp Act," March 1766, in *The Papers of Benjamin Franklin*, vol. 13, *January 1, 1766, Through December 31, 1766*, ed. Leonard W. Labaree (Yale University Press, 1969); and Benjamin Franklin to Lord Kames, February 15, 1767, in *The Papers of Benjamin Franklin*, vol. 14, *January 1, 1767, Through December 31, 1767*, ed. Leonard W. Labaree (Yale University Press, 1970), 65.

37. Clark, *The Language of Liberty*, 88; and Greene, *Constitutional Origins*, 109–10.

38. Peter D. G. Thomas, *Tea Party to Independence: The Third Phase of the American Revolution, 1773–1776* (Clarendon Press, 1991), 167–69, 174–75; and Horst Dippel, *Germany and the American Revolution, 1770–1800* (University of North Carolina Press, 1977), 73.

39. T. H. Breen, *The Will of the People: The Revolutionary Birth of America* (Belknap Press, 2021), 12.

40. Piers Mackesy, *The War for America, 1775–1783* (University of Nebraska Press, 1993), 29.

41. Armitage, *The Declaration of Independence*, 31–36, 41.

42. Scott, *British Foreign Policy in the Age of the American Revolution*, 221.

43. Larrie D. Ferreiro, *Brothers at Arms: American Independence and the Men of France and Spain Who Saved It* (Knopf, 2016), 35, 42, 54.

44. N. A. M. Rodger, *The Command of the Ocean: A Naval History of Britain, 1649–1815* (Penguin, 2005), 331; and Scott, *British Foreign Policy*, 214–15.

45. Roberts, *The Last King of America*, 273; Peter H. Wilson, *Iron and Blood: A Military History of the German-Speaking Peoples Since 1500* (Harvard University Press, 2023), 217–20; Friederike Baer, *Hessians: German Soldiers in the American Revolutionary War* (Oxford University Press, 2022), 82, 294; David M. Griffiths, "Nikita Panin, Russian Diplomacy, and the American Revolution," *Slavic Review* 28, no. 1 (1969): 4–5, https://www.jstor.org/stable/2493035; and Scott, *British Foreign Policy in the Age of the American Revolution*, 217–20, 228–30.

46. Mackesy, *The War for America, 1775–1783*, 61–62; and Baer, *Hessians*.

47. Andrew Jackson O'Shaughnessy, *The Men Who Lost America: British Leadership, the American Revolution, and the Fate of the Empire* (Yale University Press, 2014), 7.

48. Samuel Adams to Elizabeth Adams, December 9, 1776, in *Letters of Delegates to Congress, 1774–1789*, ed. Paul H. Smith (Library of Congress, 1976–2000), 5:509–10; and George Washington to Samuel Washington, December 18, 1776, Founders Online, https://founders.archives.gov/documents/Washington/03-07-02-0299.

49. Scott, *British Foreign Policy in the Age of the American Revolution*, 311–12; and George Washington to John Laurens, April 9, 1781, Library of Congress, https://www.loc.gov/resource/mgw3h.002/?sp=206.

50. Savelle, "The American Balance of Power and European Diplomacy, 1713–78," 166.

51. Ferreiro, *Brothers at Arms*, 99–100; and Dull, *A Diplomatic History of the American Revolution*, 90–94.

52. Scott, *British Foreign Policy in the Age of the American Revolution*, 268–72.

53. Kevin J. Weddle, "'A Change of Both Men and Measures': British Reassessment of Military Strategy After Saratoga, 1777–1778," *Journal of Military History* 77, no. 3 (2013): 837–65, https://www.researchgate.net/publication/291332064_A_Change_of_Both_Men_and_Measures_British_Reassessment_of_Military_Strategy_after_Saratoga_1777-1778.

54. William Anthony Hay, "An End to Empire? British Strategy in the American Revolution and in Making Peace with the United States," in *Justifying Revolution: Law, Virtue, and Violence in the American War of Independence*, ed. Glenn A. Moots and Phillip Hamilton (University of Oklahoma Press, 2017), 277.

55. David Syrett, *Neutral Rights and the War in the Narrow Seas, 1778–1782*, Combat Studies Institute, https://www.armyupress.army.mil/Portals/7/combat-studies-institute/csi-books/neutral-rights-and-the-war-in-narrow-seas-1778-82.pdf.

56. Jonathan Singerton, *The American Revolution and the Habsburg Monarchy* (University of Virginia Press, 2021), 91.

57. Bemis, *The Diplomacy of the American Revolution*, 129–31.

58. Scott, *British Foreign Policy in the Age of the American Revolution*, 303–4; Syrett, *Neutral Rights and the War in the Narrow Seas, 1778–1782*; and Isabel de Madariaga, *Britain, Russia, and the Armed Neutrality of 1780* (Hollis & Carter, 1962).

59. Dippel, *Germany and the American Revolution*, 61; and Blanning, *Frederick the Great*, 333–34.

60. Bemis, *The Diplomacy of the American Revolution*, 158–65; Griffiths, "Nikita Panin, Russian Diplomacy, and the American Revolution," 12–14, 17; and Singerton, *The American Revolution and the Habsburg Monarchy*, 133–34.

61. Scott, *British Foreign Policy in the Age of the American Revolution*, 314–16.

62. O'Shaughnessy, *The Men Who Lost America*, 3.

63. Dull, *A Diplomatic History of the American Revolution*, 139–51, 158–60, 170–71.

64. Angelo M. Codevilla, *America's Rise and Fall Among Nations: Lessons in Statecraft from John Quincy Adams* (Encounter Books, 2022), 24–25.

65. Armitage, *The Declaration of Independence*, 85–88.

66. Franco Venturi, *The End of the Old Regime in Europe, 1776–1789, Part I: The Great States of the West*, trans. R. Burr Litchfield (Princeton University Press, 1991), 4, 13, 17–18.

67. Singerton, *The American Revolution and the Habsburg Monarchy*, 51–53.

68. J. H. Elliott, *Empires of the Atlantic World: Britain and Spain in America, 1492–1830* (Yale University Press, 2006), 367–68.

69. Schroeder, *The Transformation of European Politics, 1763–1848*, 39.

70. Quoted in T. C. W. Blanning, "'That Horrid Electorate' or 'Ma Patrie Germanique'? George III, Hanover, and the *Fürstenbund* of 1785," *Historical Journal* 20, no. 2 (1977): 314–15, https://www.cambridge.org/core/journals/historical-journal/article/abs/that-horrid-electorate-or-ma-patrie-germanique-george-iii-hanover-and-the-furstenbund-of-1785/1E914CA52E676A96428CF0B8602A48A4; George III to Lord North, June 13, 1781, in *The Correspondence of King George III from 1760 to December 1783*,

ed. John Fortescue (Frank Cass, 1967), 5:247; Earl of Buckingham to Sir Henry Clinton, December 1781, in *Report on the Manuscripts of the Marquess of Lothian Preserved at Blickling Hall, Norfolk* (Wyman and Sons, 1905), 404; Singerton, *The American Revolution and the Habsburg Monarchy*, 50; and Scott, *British Foreign Policy in the Age of the American Revolution*, 339.

71. P. J. Marshall, *Remaking the British Atlantic: The United States and the British Empire After American Independence* (Oxford University Press, 2012), 17.

72. *The Parliamentary Register* [. . .], vol. 21 (London, 1787), 176–77.

73. Franco Venturi, *The End of the Old Regime in Europe, 1768–1776: The First Crisis*, trans. R. Burr Litchfield (Princeton University Press, 1989), ix–xii.

74. Schroeder, *The Transformation of European Politics, 1763–1848*, 6–10.

75. Simon Schama, *Citizens: A Chronicle of the French Revolution* (Knopf, 1989), 24–31, 43–48; and David A. Bell, *Men on Horseback: The Power of Charisma in the Age of Revolutions* (Farrar, Straus and Giroux, 2020), 73–76.

76. Armitage, *The Declaration of Independence*, 113–14; and Robert A. Kann, *A History of the Habsburg Empire, 1526–1918* (University of California Press, 1974), 205–7.

77. John Adams, *Discourses on Davila* [. . .] (Boston, 1805).

78. Friedrich von Gentz, *The Origins and Principles of the American Revolution Compared with the Origins and Principles of the French Revolution*, trans. John Quincy Adams (Liberty Fund, 2010).

79. *The Works of John Adams, Second President of the United States*, ed. Charles Francis Adams (Boston, 1856), 10:505.

80. George C. Herring, *From Colony to Superpower: U.S. Foreign Relations Since 1776* (Oxford University Press, 2008), 68–73; Lindsay M. Chervinsky, *The Cabinet: George Washington and the Creation of an American Institution* (Harvard University Press, 2020); and Morton J. Frisch, ed. *The Pacificus–Helvidius Debates, 1793–1794* (Liberty Fund, 2007).

81. Howard W. Cox, *American Traitor: General James Wilkinson's Betrayal of the Republic and Escape from Justice* (Georgetown University Press, 2023).

82. Edmund Randolph to George Hammond, May 1, 1794, in *American State Papers*, class 1, *Foreign Relations*, ed. Walter Lowrie and Matthew St. Clair Clarke (Washington, DC, 1832–61), 1:451–52.

83. Robert H. Ferrell, *American Diplomacy: A History* (W. W. Norton, 1979), 87–93.

84. Francis D. Cogliano, *Emperor of Liberty: Thomas Jefferson's Foreign Policy* (Yale University Press, 2014), 71, 679.

85. C. A. Bayly, *Imperial Meridian: The British Empire and the World, 1780–1830* (Longman Group, 1989), 72–73.

86. Gentz, *The Origins and Principles of the American Revolution* [. . .]; and Friedrich von Gentz, "Mémoire," in Historical Manuscripts Commission, *Report on the Manuscripts of J. B. Fortescue, Esq., Preserved at Dropmore* (John Falconer, 1908), 6:375.

87. A. D. Harvey, *Collisions of Empires: Britain in Three World Wars, 1793–1945* (Bloomsbury Academic, 1991).

88. Cogliano, *Emperor of Liberty*, 3.

89. Dominic Lieven, *Russia Against Napoleon: The True Story of the Campaigns of War and Peace* (Viking, 2010), 70.

90. Harvey, *Collision of Empires*, 101.

91. Lieven, *Russia Against Napoleon*, 16–17.

92. J. P. Riley links the two wars in 1813 as parts of a larger global conflict in J. P. Riley, *Napoleon and the World War of 1813: Lessons in Coalition Warfighting* (Frank Cass, 2000).

93. McDougall, *Promised Land, Crusader State*, 35–36.

94. Elliott, *Empires of the Atlantic World*, 364–65.

95. Schroeder, *The Transformation of European Politics, 1763–1848*, 340–43.

96. Elliott, *Empires of the Atlantic World*, 395–96.

97. Armitage, *The Declaration of Independence*, 115–16, 118–21.

98. *Federalist*, no. 51 (James Madison); and Samuel P. Huntington, *Political Order in Changing Societies* (Yale University Press, 1968), 7.

99. John Quincy Adams to John Adams, December 21, 1817, in *Writings of John Quincy Adams*, ed. Worthington Chauncey Ford (Macmillan, 1916), 6:276.

100. Elliott, *Empires of the Atlantic World*, 393–94; and Schroeder, *The Transformation of European Politics, 1763–1848*, 630–34.

101. Schroeder, *The Transformation of European Politics, 1763–1848*, 634.

102. Charles N. Edel, *Nation Builder: John Quincy Adams and the Grand Strategy of the Republic* (Harvard University Press, 2014), 168–80.

103. I take this phrase from Fareed Zakaria, *From Wealth to Power: The Unusual Origins of America's World Role* (Princeton University Press, 1999).

104. John Quincy Adams to Richard C. Anderson, May 27, 1823, in *Writings of John Quincy Adams*, 7:460.

2

The Law of Nations and the
Founding of the American Nation

JEREMY RABKIN

Amid the Mexican Revolution in the early 20th century, an American journalist secured an interview with the rebel general Pancho Villa. The journalist asked Villa what he thought of the recent Hague Convention on the law of war. Villa, "hugely amused," called it "a funny thing to make rules about war."[1]

One might imagine the leaders of the American Revolution, more than a century earlier, expressing comparable disdain for the notion that European rules could govern the conduct of American militiamen then fighting the British army. One might imagine American leaders would have dismissed any European rules constraining their struggle for independence.

But the American founders were, in fact, quite attentive to American obligations under the law of nations (as international law was then called). That is evident from what American leaders said and did from the Revolution's outset. It is even clearer from debates about adopting a new constitution, soon after the United States secured independence. It is equally clear from the conduct of American diplomacy in the ensuing decades.

One reason the founders were so devoted to international law is that they saw it as largely conforming to principles and premises Americans accepted at home. Where there were differences, they pressed to get other governments to embrace American views of what international practice should be.

Revolution According to Law

The American Revolution's most famous document—the Declaration of Independence—starts and ends with appeals to international law. Today, the Declaration is most often remembered for its second paragraph, asserting the "self-evident" truths that "all men are created equal," endowed with "unalienable Rights." But the first sentence—"When in the Course of human events"—argues that it is the "Laws of Nature and of Nature's God" that "entitle" an independent America, "among the powers of the earth," to a "separate and equal station."

That initial claim might seem more a philosophical speculation than an agreed rule of international law. But the closing sentence then asserts, with much more specificity, that "as Free and Independent States," the United States "have full Power to levy War, conclude Peace, contract Alliances, establish Commerce, and to do all other Acts and Things which Independent States may of right do." It is a claim about not only powers inherent in statehood but also implied limits: Some "Acts and Things" would not be right for states to do. Was this, too, just philosophical speculation?

For the American founders (and many authorities in Europe), there was no sharp distinction between principles of natural law and the law invoked by practicing lawyers. Certainly that was true in regard to international law. By far the most widely cited work on that subject in that era was the treatise of the Swiss diplomat Emer de Vattel, *The Law of Nations*, which had first appeared (in French, as *Le Droit des Gens*) in 1758. The subtitle illustrates the prevailing view: *The Principles of Natural Law Applied to the Conduct and to the Affairs of Nations and of Sovereigns.*

We know the Revolution's leaders were familiar with Vattel. Benjamin Franklin requested that Vattel's publisher send several copies of his work to the Continental Congress, and they were then widely circulated there.[2] It may be that Thomas Jefferson was inspired to write about "Life, Liberty, and the pursuit of Happiness" from a passage in Vattel's treatise, asserting each man's need "by nature of becoming better, and therefore happier."[3]

Certainly the drafters of the Declaration would have drawn confidence from Vattel's explanation of the natural equality of states:

> Since men are by nature equal, . . . Nations . . . are by nature equal and hold from nature the same obligations and the same rights. . . . A dwarf is as much a man as a giant is; a small Republic is no less a sovereign State than the most powerful Kingdom.[4]

That was one major reason why American leaders were keen to invoke prevailing ideas about the law of nations—that they supported the claim of their new, struggling confederation to the same status as well-established states of Europe ("separate and equal station" "among the powers of the earth"). Appeals to the law of nations might also reinforce protests against British abuses, exceeding what states could "of right do"—such as unleashing "merciless Indian Savages" who attacked women and children or deploying German mercenaries who plundered and ransacked civilian towns, reverting to practices of "the most barbarous ages."[5] Vattel's treatise (among others) decried such practices and supported a presumptive or natural claim to engage in trade (corresponding to the Declaration's protest against Britain for "cutting off our Trade with all parts of the world"). Beyond all that, Vattel's treatise stipulated that oppressed people had a natural right to resist tyranny and seek foreign assistance for their efforts.[6]

The Continental Congress, which issued the Declaration, wanted recognition from the "candid world" to which the Declaration was addressed. The Congress hoped the Declaration's argument might help persuade the British to acknowledge American independence. It might make European governments and European bankers more willing to advance loans to the struggling American confederation. And it might open the way to favorable trade agreements with European states.

So, in the summer of 1776, as John Adams was consulting with Jefferson on the Declaration of Independence's text, he was working up a draft for a model trade treaty. The Congress then approved plans for a trade treaty with France (and whatever other governments in Europe that might want to agree to one). It was already a proposal for liberalizing trade, beyond generally accepted practices. But the treaty negotiated with France in 1778 largely followed its provisions, as France was particularly keen to help the embattled new nation. It signed a military alliance shortly after.

The trade treaty's most notable elements were provisions to protect commerce from disruption in wartime (among other things, protections for neutral shipping) and to protect signatories from foreign rivalries (with a most-favored-nation clause assuring further concessions as generous as those granted to any future trade partner). Some 50 years later, John Quincy Adams (then serving as US secretary of state) claimed that the model treaty ought to be ranked with the Declaration of Independence as "parts of one and the same system": The trade treaty was "to the foundation of our commercial intercourse with the rest of mankind, what the Declaration of Independence was to that of our internal Government."[7]

In its early years, however, the United States had only limited success in negotiating similar treaties with other European states. In particular, it could not secure a trade agreement with Britain, even after it recognized American independence—a particular disappointment given that most American trade had centered on Britain in colonial times and might again with supportive agreements. Even after conceding American independence, however, Britain declined for some time to make a generous trade agreement. In part, it held back to protest the United States' failures to honor commitments in the 1783 treaty that ended the War of Independence.

One of the principal arguments for the new federal Constitution was the need to strengthen America's capacity to deal with foreign nations. Of the first dozen Federalist Papers, nine concern international trade or international security. *Federalist* 12, for example, argues that a newly empowered Congress could raise effective tariffs on foreign imports, while separate state tariffs could be easily evaded by unloading foreign cargoes in a neighboring state. That broad federal tariff power could then be wielded to induce foreign states to enter generous trade agreements.

Among notable provisions of the Constitution, Article VI made treaties (along with federal statutes) "supreme Law of the Land," while
Article III, Section 2 gave jurisdiction to federal courts to interpret and
uphold them—to avoid states inadvertently offending foreign powers
by disregarding American treaty obligations. Similarly, the obligation to
protect foreign diplomats was safeguarded with provisions in Article III
giving federal courts authority over cases concerning such diplomats and
allowing the Supreme Court to hear such cases in original jurisdiction
(that is, without the delay and possible provocation of lower court trials).
By Article I, Section 8, Congress was given power to enact penalties for
"Offences against the Law of Nations," so the US could take its part in
upholding the law of nations.[8]

As it turned out, the new federal government was no sooner organized
than it faced major foreign challenges. Most threatening were the French
Revolution and the ensuing wars between France and its neighbors, especially Britain. France and Britain eventually tried to block trade with each
other (and third parties trying to trade with the other). The neutral United
States argued strongly against these practices as contrary to (what it saw
as) accepted international law. The United States even more vehemently
opposed the British and French practices of interfering with neutral ships
on the high seas to enforce these trade restrictions.

President George Washington borrowed a copy of Vattel's treatise from
a library in New York, most likely to sort through these and related challenges. He did not return it, perhaps because these challenges continued,
even when the national capital moved to Philadelphia.[9] His secretary of
state, Jefferson, produced several state papers on neutral states' rights
and obligations in international trade. European governments cited them
respectfully decades later.[10]

The European war was still raging, and still threatening American
trade, when Jefferson became president. His secretary of state, James
Madison, wrote a book-length study aimed at refuting British claims of
a right to interfere with neutral shipping, reviewing doctrines of Vattel
and earlier European commentators, notably Hugo Grotius, Samuel von

Pufendorf, and Jean-Jacques Burlamaqui, along with court rulings from various nations on related issues.[11] As Madison probably expected, it did not persuade British authorities to change their policies. But it may confirm the general point, that the founders took international law seriously enough to appeal to it in foreign affairs and try to influence the general understanding of what it required.

Meanwhile, as the founders had expected, many issues involving foreign relations came before federal courts. The Supreme Court in the era of Chief Justice John Marshall (1801–35) is most remembered today for foundational rulings interpreting the Constitution. But the Marshall Court actually handed down three times as many rulings dealing with international law as US constitutional law (195 international cases to 62 constitutional cases).[12] Today's Supreme Court still cites a number of Marshall's opinions on international law, and foreign courts have cited some with approval.[13]

The first extended treatise on American law—James Kent's *Commentaries on American Law*, first published in 1826—also deserves notice. Kent, who started his career as a protégé of Alexander Hamilton in New York, was a nationally renowned jurist (serving on high courts in New York) by the time he gave the lectures gathered in this treatise. Half of the first volume (of four) was devoted to a survey of the law of nations, drawing heavily on Vattel but then reviewing relevant decisions of the Marshall Court and state courts that regarded the law of nations (or some parts of it, such as rules concerning the treatment of foreign ambassadors and foreign ships) as part of the common law. Kent's *Commentaries*, superseding William Blackstone's mid-18th-century *Commentaries on the Law of England*, remained a leading text for American law students to the end of the 19th century.

So the founding generations took international law seriously. But they were not naive about what it could be expected to achieve.

Guarded Expectations

The founders regarded "the law of nations" as a guide to *proper* conduct between states. That did not mean they trusted that states would always conform to it. Early American statesmen tended to view the law of nations as a set of background expectations that might allow for adjustment or exceptions over time. They were quite aware that it remained a law governing sovereigns, and sovereigns could not be readily coerced by legal argument. That was one of the main arguments for authorizing direct federal control over private conduct in some areas, since state governments could not be trusted to do so based on mere admonitions by the central government.[14]

Outside the United States' special constitutional structure, the framers assumed sovereign states would usually give more weight to their own self-interest when interpreting or applying supposed international obligations. As John Jay, an experienced diplomat, warned in an early Federalist Paper, "It is well known that [in international disputes,] acknowledgments, explanations, and compensations are often accepted as satisfactory from a strong nation, which would be rejected as unsatisfactory if offered by a State or confederacy of little consideration or power."[15] As Hamilton warned in a later paper, "The rights of neutrality will only be respected when they are defended by an adequate power."[16] He offered this as a key reason for establishing a federal government with resources to build an American navy, capable of protecting American shipping on the high seas.

Such "realism" was already evident in the conduct of American diplomacy. To take a telling example, the Treaty of Alliance with France in 1778 promised that neither signatory would negotiate a separate peace with Britain and that both would maintain peaceful relations thereafter.[17] Even during the war, however, Washington warned against embracing any military project that would see French troops deployed to Canada. The French, he cautioned, might decide to remain there and eventually prove a threat to American independence.[18]

Later on, American diplomats did engage in separate peace negotiations with British emissaries. France's foreign minister, when informed of this development, protested that it violated the obligation of coordinated action stipulated in the Treaty of Alliance. Jay, one of the American negotiators in Paris, explained to the Continental Congress that the American emissaries "were determined faithfully to fulfil our Treaty [with France], *yet it was a different thing to be guided by their or our Construction of it.*"[19] (Emphasis in original.)

After securing independence—with decisive French support—the United States soon found itself faced with more awkward challenges arising from the French treaty. Did it mean the United States was obliged to stand by France in the wars that broke out after the French Revolution? President Washington, relying on a narrow interpretation of the treaty, proclaimed American neutrality. There was much domestic debate on whether the president could make this determination on his own, a dispute engaging Madison and Hamilton on opposite sides of an ensuing pamphlet war (between Hamilton's "Pacificus" papers and Madison's replies as "Helvidius"). But there was not much controversy about the policy's substance. When President Adams subsequently negotiated a new treaty with France, absolving the United States of further obligations, the Senate endorsed it with notably little opposition.[20]

Within a mere two decades thereafter, the United States extended its reach as far as the Pacific. It might not have been able to if it had been extremely scrupulous about international legalities. In 1803, the Jefferson administration accepted France's offer to sell a vast swath of territory on the far side of the Mississippi—following French Foreign Minister Charles Maurice de Talleyrand-Périgord's suggestion not to look too closely into France's claim to have clear title to this territory (rather than Spain, the previous owner). Fifteen years later, General Andrew Jackson marched into Spain's colony in Florida to suppress raids by local Indians into neighboring American territory. Jackson then asserted authority to hang two British nationals accused of arming and inciting Indians in Florida. Secretary of State John Quincy Adams defended these legally questionable actions and warned of further measures if Spain did not relinquish this territory that it seemed unable to control. Spain agreed to sell Florida to the United States.

Soon after, further pressure won Spain's acceptance of American claims to extend its Louisiana territory to the Pacific coast, at least north of Spain's province of California. Still, it is notable that the United States wanted to settle its claims with formal treaties, often (as with the acquisition of Florida) by paying monetary compensation. American diplomacy sought to show that territorial cessions were not merely the result of force (even if the threat of force might have played some role in closing the bargain).

The United States was willing to see lawyers (not merely diplomats) take a role in settling disputes—but with safeguards. Thus, in 1794, Washington sent Jay, now chief justice, to negotiate a treaty with Britain to resolve lingering disputes arising from the War of Independence. Among other things, the Jay Treaty provided for arbitration panels to settle property claims by Tory loyalists whose property had been confiscated in America and by American merchants claiming that the British had wrongly seized their property. It was the first modern venture in international arbitration. Some critics questioned whether this could be consistent with the Constitution's entrusting "the judicial Power of the United States" to federal courts—an argument advanced at the time by the new congressman from the new state of Tennessee, Andrew Jackson.[21]

But the precedent established was not merely to allow arbitration panels to obligate American government payments but also to require Senate agreement, with a separate international convention, to the issues thus submitted—a practice honored down to the mid-20th century. As president, Jackson would commend France for agreeing to pay compensation for depredations against American commerce (back in the 1790s) without arbitration of individual claims—though by then accepting that this could be a lawful resort.[22]

Other ventures in international decision-making were still resisted. Notably, Congress agreed in 1808 to prohibit the importation of slaves to the United States, and the US Navy was assigned to patrol Atlantic waters to stop slave trading. But when Britain proposed that an international tribunal judge charges of slave trading, the United States declined to participate. There were again constitutional concerns that such a tribunal would, in effect, be exercising American judicial authority—not merely (as with the Jay Treaty panels) by financial awards against the Treasury but by direct prosecution of private (and possibly American) citizens. Some opposition may have reflected slave states' concerns, but the leading opponent of the scheme was Secretary of State Adams, who would prove himself in later years a principled opponent of slavery.[23]

As president, Adams resisted American participation in a congress of newly independent Latin states unless it was made clear it would not establish a hemispheric authority compromising American independence. The wrangling on this point was so extended that by the time American delegates were authorized to attend—with emphatic cautions to act only as observers—the conference had already broken up.[24]

Whatever other diplomatic or political considerations may have influenced these stands, Adams had powerful logic on his side. Americans had fought a war to establish their independence and another war, starting in 1812, to make sure Britain would respect it. There was therefore understandable wariness about placing America under any foreign or even multinational constraint. American legal commentators were among the first to embrace the new term "international law"—coined precisely to emphasize that this law was about relations between states, not more generalized norms that many states happened to regard as moral or proper.[25] The early American republic sought from the beginning to champion what it regarded as just or favorable doctrines of international law, but always with the understanding that they would respect America's own constitutional structure.

Even as that structure was debated, Madison in the Federalist Papers praised the constitutional provision allowing the federal government to protect the states from "invasion" and "domestic violence." He even voiced the wistful thought that it would be a "happy" result "if a project equally effectual could be established for the universal peace of mankind"—but then dismissed such a "project" as "chimerical."[26] As he noted in a later paper, "A power independent of the society may as well espouse the unjust views of the major, as the rightful interest of the minor party, and may possibly be turned against both parties."[27]

Madison elaborated the thought a few years later, in a 1792 essay on "Universal Peace" in which he noted that Jean-Jacques Rousseau's proposal for a European peace federation, guaranteeing every member state's territory and authority, would have "the tendency . . . to perpetuate arbitrary power wherever it existed; and, by extinguishing the hope of one day seeing an end of oppression, to cut off the only source of consolation remaining to the oppressed."[28] The point hardly needed elaborating for readers of that era. They would have been well aware that America had gained its independence by defying the British Empire's peace and territorial integrity. They would have shuddered at the thought that all the European powers could have been obligated to safeguard all Britain's territorial claims as they happened to exist in 1776.

But that was all long ago. Does the United States still need to worry about overreaching international projects? Does it need to care much about validation from other nations?

Contemporary Resonance

The United States' situation in its earliest years was quite different, of course, from today. The early United States, a string of small states along the Atlantic Seaboard, faced threats from powerful colonial empires—British, French, Spanish—on its borders or in its immediate vicinity. It faced formidable trade barriers with major states in Europe. It faced serious threats to its shipping on the high seas. In the 21st century, with a hundred times the population, with territory from the mid-Pacific to the Caribbean basin, and with the world's largest economy, the United States is a superpower. Do we need to care quite as much about international law?

There are obvious reasons to think so. Almost by definition, a superpower has interests stretching far beyond its neighborhood. We seek trade relations with countries around the world and security arrangements—including agreements on hosting American troops, warships, and airfields—in foreign lands. It is a natural instinct of smaller states to be wary of great powers, so it is a particular challenge for a superpower to win allies' and partners' trust. Demonstrating respect for treaty commitments and international law obligations is one important way of cultivating trust.

The point hardly needs belaboring, as a general rule. The United States gains trust by showing that it is trustworthy. There may be necessary or justifiable exceptions to our adherence to international law—even to our own understanding of it—in special circumstances. As Madison noted, in a case of "absolute necessity," the "great principle of self-preservation" must prevail; "the transcendent law of nature and of nature's God" declares "all institutions must be sacrificed" to "the safety and happiness of society."[29] The founders would not likely have seen threatening force to annex Greenland or the Panama Canal (in current circumstances) as excused by absolute necessity.

But it is worth noticing that the founders did not simply focus on the foreign policy benefits of adhering to acceptable conduct in foreign relations. They were also interested in how American conduct toward foreign nations would affect Americans' views of their own government or country.

So, within days of the signing of the peace treaty ending the American War of Independence, John Adams, one of the three American negotiators, wrote to the president of the Continental Congress, urging that

> Congress ought in all their proceedings to consider, the Opinion that the United States or the People of America will entertain of themselves. We may call this national Vanity or national Pride, but it is the main Principle of the national Sense of its own Dignity and a Passion in human Nature, without which nations cannot preserve the Character of Men.[30]

Adams accordingly urged renewed efforts to secure diplomatic representation at the Austrian and Russian imperial courts to reassure Americans of their new country's status, even if it secured no concrete commercial advantage.[31]

A few years later, Hamilton made a similar point at the Constitutional Convention:

> It had been said that respectability in the eyes of foreign Nations was not the object at which we aimed; that the proper object of republican Government was domestic tranquility & happiness. This was an ideal distinction. No Governmt. could give us tranquility & happiness at home, which did not possess sufficient stability and strength to make us respectable abroad.[32]

What did he mean by "respectable"? Among other things, the capacity to keep promises and conform to a reliable course of conduct despite temptations or threats. So Madison, in the Federalist Papers, warned that the United States was now "held in no respect by her friends" and would become "prey to every nation which has an interest in speculating on her fluctuating councils and embarrassed affairs."[33] Yet "every government" would find it "desirable" that its actions "should appear to other nations as the offspring of a wise and honorable policy."[34] The argument is actually part of a more general argument for the benefits of a senate with more seasoned members, giving more foresight and stability to the government. The application to foreign affairs is merely one illustration of the argument, but Madison seemed to regard it as a particularly compelling one, as foreigners' disdain might seem particularly demoralizing (and dangerous).

International law could supplement other brakes on impulsive action. So in Washington's second term, Hamilton defended Washington's neutrality policy in a pamphlet that argued against treating France's aid in the Revolution as a claim on enduring American friendship, noting that when one nation bestows benefits on another, the benefactor's "predominant motive" is "the interest or advantage of the [bestowing] Nation." But he was then quick to disclaim the idea that America should adopt "a policy absolutely selfish," urging Americans instead to embrace "a policy regulated by their own interest, *as far as justice and good faith permit.*"[35] (Emphasis added.)

A few years later, critics in Congress were furious at the Adams administration for agreeing to extradite an American citizen accused of murder on a British ship. Critics demanded that, rather than extradite the accused to British authorities, the sailor be tried by Americans in an American court. A Virginia congressman gave such a masterful account of why this would be contrary to the law of nations that Adams appointed that congressman—the young John Marshall—secretary of state and then chief justice.[36] Many of Marshall's subsequent Supreme Court decisions limited the reach of American power in deference to the law of nations, particularly in regard to actions against foreign ships on the high seas. These rulings may have reassured foreign powers, but they also made the point to Americans that the United States respects established law, even in dealing with foreign states.

It is probably still true today, as in the first decades of our history, that a government that acts in international affairs as if power is the only limit on its actions will risk undermining its own citizens' confidence in its trustworthiness at home. The effect may be illustrated by the drop in public support (at least as measured by opinion polls) for the aggressive and seemingly erratic tariff policy initiated in the first months of the second Trump administration. Even many of those who hoped for economic benefits seem to have felt some alarm that such extreme measures could be launched, with only the most tenuous basis in domestic law and with entire disregard for international trade agreements, previously accepted as legally binding on the United States.

The founders looked to the law of nations not only as a brake on impulsive action, however, but also as a potential basis for mobilizing American opinion for hard measures, including resort to war. Thus, when Madison urged Congress to declare war on Britain in 1812, he rehearsed the abusive British practices—interfering with American shipping on the high seas (and conscripting captured American citizens into the service of the Royal Navy)—depicting them as clear violations of international law. But the legal argument was then used to launch a more primal appeal to national self-respect. There could be no further delay in deploying force, Madison warned,

> without breaking down the spirit of the nation, destroying all confidence in itself and in its political institutions and either perpetuating a state of disgraceful suffering or regaining by more costly sacrifices and more severe struggle our lost rank and respect among independent nations.[37]

Such rhetoric may seem far from the technical legal parsing of treaties or accepted international practice that legal specialists now present as international law. But statesmen of the early republic did not make a sharp distinction between "law" and "justice and good faith" (to adopt Hamilton's phrase). And intensive legal analysis does not completely displace citizens' more general expectation—or, at least, hope—that their government will act in ways that are justifiable and legitimate, worthy of foreign states' respect. Perhaps putting it that way slips from precise legal claims to generalized claims of honor or reputation. But it was hardly whimsy or superstition that led early American statesmen to make such associations.

Honor, Nature, and Law

The United States began with a war for independence. But independence is a complicated, almost paradoxical idea. When still living alone on his island refuge, Robinson Crusoe had no need to proclaim his independence any more than to assert property rights or trading privileges. In international affairs, as in private life, independence is relational. It does not confer a right to follow any impulse that arises. It is the right to do what is rightful or generally accepted as such.

Eighteenth-century thinkers and commentators expressed this thought by positing that in the state of nature, where there is no government, there is still a law of nature limiting what individuals may do to others. Vattel, borrowing from Locke, insisted that independent nations remained in a state of nature with each other but were still bound by certain principles of proper conduct (particularly regarding avoidance of aggression).[38] This was common wisdom in founding-era writings.

Where there are no reliable courts, individuals must make their own efforts to assert their rights. They are unlikely to do so effectively, however, if constantly quarreling with neighbors even on small matters. To have the confidence to assert one's rights—in the absence of courts and sheriffs—requires something beyond legalistic doctrines, something once called character or honor. Harsh necessities may still claim priority in extreme situations. But in extreme situations, there is more room for doubt about what conduct is justifiable. It helps if one can invoke a good reputation earned by decent practice in the general run of situations, even amid pressures and temptations. It helps to be recognized as honorable.

The Declaration of Independence opens with a sentence appealing to what is "necessary." But the Declaration's last word—literally the very last word of the text—is "honor." The signatories appealed not to the achievements of battlefield commanders but to political leaders' honor, justifying their defiance of constituted authority (and the regular claims of legality) with arguments from natural law and the law of nations.

Notes

1. Margaret MacMillan, *War: How Conflict Shaped Us* (Random House, 2020), 205–6.
2. Franklin wrote, "I am much obliged by the kind present you have made us of your edition of Vattel. It came to us in good season, when the circumstances of a rising state make it necessary frequently to consult the law of nations. Accordingly, that copy . . . has been continually in the hands of the members of our congress." Benjamin Franklin to Charles-Guillaume-Frédéric Dumas, December 9, 1775, Founders

Online, https://founders.archives.gov/documents/Franklin/01-22-02-0172. Dumas had just published a new edition of Vattel's treatise in the Netherlands. He would go on to publish translations of the American Declaration of Independence and early state constitutions, becoming an unofficial publicist for the American cause. The National Archives website Founders Online includes more than 50 letters from Franklin to Dumas in 1775–89, mostly to inform Dumas of American diplomatic initiatives.

3. Emer de Vattel, *The Law of Nations*, trans. Charles G. Fenwick (1758; Carnegie Institution of Washington, 1916), vol. 1, chap. 2, sec. 21.

4. Vattel, *The Law of Nations*, introduction, sec. 18.

5. It was at least partly to uphold the Continental Army's reputation as a reputable and honorable force that General Washington insisted on treating British (and Hessian) prisoners of war in accord with European standards of proper care. David Hackett Fischer, *Washington's Crossing* (Oxford University Press, 2004), 378–79.

6. "A Nation may depose a tyrant and refuse obedience to him." Vattel, *The Law of Nations*, bk. 1, chap. 4, sec. 51. In civil war or contest over domestic authority, other states may "assist the party which seems to have justice on its side, should that party ask for help." Vattel, *The Law of Nations*, bk. 3, chap. 18, sec. 296.

7. John Quincy Adams, "Extracts from Mr Adams' Instructions to Mr Anderson, Minister Plenipotentiary to Colombia, Dated 27th May, 1823," in Jonathan Elliot, *The American Diplomatic Code* [. . .] (Washington, DC, 1834), 652. Colombia was the first of the new Latin American republics with which the United States exchanged diplomatic envoys, so the instructions to Anderson were expected to serve as a model for subsequent diplomatic ventures in the Americas.

8. US Const. art. VI; US Const. art. III, § 2; and US Const. art. I, § 8.

9. New York Society Library, "Historic Mount Vernon Returns Copy of Rare Book Borrowed by George Washington in 1789 to the New York Society Library," May 21, 2010, https://www.nysoclib.org/historic-mount-vernon-returns-copy-rare-book-borrowed-george-washington-1789-new-york-society. The library does not seem to have tried to collect fines for the late return.

10. For example, British Foreign Secretary George Canning said, "If I wished for a guide in a system of neutrality, I should take that laid down by America in the days of the presidency of Washington, and the secretaryship of Jefferson. . . . Here, Sir, I contend is the principle of neutrality upon which we ought to act." HC Deb. (2d ser.) (16 Apr. 1823) (8) cols. 1056–57.

11. James Madison, *An Examination of the British Doctrine Which Subjects to Capture a Neutral Trade, Not Open in Time of Peace* (London, 1806).

12. J. B. Moore, "John Marshall," *Political Science Quarterly* 16, no. 3 (1901): 402, 405, https://www.jstor.org/stable/pdf/2140254.pdf.

13. For a concise overview highlighting major decisions, see David L. Sloss et al., eds., *International Law in the U.S. Supreme Court* (Cambridge University Press, 2011), chap. 1.

14. For example, European schemes to secure

> the peace of that part of the world . . . [give] an instructive but afflicting lesson to mankind, how little dependence is to be placed on treaties

which have no other sanction than the obligations of good faith . . . to [restrain] the impulse of any immediate interest or passion. . . .

. . . There is, in the nature of sovereign power, an impatience of control, that disposes those who are invested with the exercise of it, to look with an evil eye upon all external attempts to restrain or direct its operations.

Federalist, no. 15 (Alexander Hamilton).

15. *Federalist*, no. 3 (John Jay).

16. *Federalist*, no. 11 (Alexander Hamilton).

17. Treaty of Alliance Between the United States of America and His Most Christian Majesty, Fr.-U.S., Feb. 6, 1778, 8 Stat. 6.

18. George Washington to Henry Laurens, November 14, 1778, Founders Online, https://founders.archives.gov/documents/Washington/03-18-02-0147.

19. John Jay to Robert R. Livingston, November 17, 1782, Founders Online, https://founders.archives.gov/documents/Jay/01-03-02-0076.

20. Lawrence S. Kaplan, *Colonies into Nation: American Diplomacy, 1763–1801* (Macmillan, 1972), chap. 10.

21. US Const., art. III, § 1; and Andrew Jackson to Nathaniel Macon, October 4, 1795. Jackson was protesting against the Jay Treaty for (among other things) "erecting courts not heard of in the Constitution."

22. Andrew Jackson, "Third Annual Message to Congress," December 6, 1831, https://millercenter.org/the-presidency/presidential-speeches/december-6-1831-third-annual-message-congress. When France delayed in delivering payment, Jackson threatened to confiscate French property in the United States to provide satisfaction—despite American appreciation of France's "liberal institutions" since its 1830 revolution: "In maintaining our national rights and honor all governments are alike to us." Andrew Jackson, "Sixth Annual Message to Congress," December 1, 1834, https://millercenter.org/the-presidency/presidential-speeches/december-1-1834-sixth-annual-message-congress.

23. Eugene Kontorovich, "The Constitutionality of International Courts: The Forgotten Precedent of Slave-Trade Tribunals," *University of Pennsylvania Law Review* 158, no. 1 (2009): 39–115, https://scholarship.law.upenn.edu/cgi/viewcontent.cgi?article=1123&context=penn_law_review.

24. "The assembly will be in its nature diplomatic and not legislative; nothing can be transacted there obligatory upon any one of the States to be represented at the meeting, unless . . . subject to the ratification of its constitutional authority at home." John Quincy Adams to House of Representatives, March 15, 1826, American Presidency Project, https://www.presidency.ucsb.edu/documents/special-message-104. For an overview of the dispute, see David Currie, *The Constitution in Congress*, vol. 2, *The Jeffersonians, 1801–1829* (University of Chicago Press, 2000), 212–16.

25. In a book published in 1789, English legal reformer Jeremy Bentham urged that "law of nations" should be replaced by the new term "international law" to make clear

that it dealt with "mutual transactions between sovereigns" rather than shared practices in "internal jurisprudence." Jeremy Bentham, *An Introduction to the Principles of Morals and Legislation* (London, 1789), chap. 17, para. 25. Henry Wheaton's *Elements of International Law* (1836) was the first full-length treatise in English adopting this term. Wheaton had been court reporter to the US Supreme Court (1816–27) before serving as a US diplomat in Europe and shared his treatises with Marshall.

26. *Federalist*, no. 43 (James Madison).

27. *Federalist*, no. 51 (James Madison).

28. James Madison, "Universal Peace," *National Gazette*, February 2, 1792, https://founders.archives.gov/documents/Madison/01-14-02-0185.

29. *Federalist*, no. 43 (Madison). Madison paraphrased the Declaration of Independence to make a more general point.

30. John Adams to Elias Boudinot, September 5, 1783, in *Papers of John Adams*, vol. 15, *June 1783–January 1784*, ed. Gregg L. Lint et al. (Massachusetts Historical Society, 2010), 255.

31. Adams to Boudinot.

32. Alexander Hamilton, speech, June 29, 1787, in *Records of the Federal Convention of 1787*, ed. Max Farrand (Yale University Press, 1937), 1:466–67.

33. *Federalist*, no. 62 (James Madison).

34. *Federalist*, no. 63 (James Madison).

35. Alexander Hamilton, "Pacificus No. IV," July 10, 1793, Founders Online, https://founders.archives.gov/documents/Hamilton/01-15-02-0066.

36. For background on this dispute, see Ruth Wedgwood, "The Revolutionary Martyrdom of Jonathan Robbins," *Yale Law Journal* 100, no. 2 (1990): 229–368, https://www.jstor.org/stable/796618.

37. James Madison, "Special Message to Congress on the Foreign Policy Crisis—War Message," June 1, 1812, https://millercenter.org/the-presidency/presidential-speeches/june-1-1812-special-message-congress-foreign-policy-crisis-war.

38. Independent states "may be regarded as so many free persons living together in a state of nature." Vattel, *The Law of Nations*, introduction, sec. 12. "He who enters upon a war for motives of gain only, without justifying grounds, acts without any right, and wages an unjust war." Vattel, *The Law of Nations*, bk. 3, chap. 3, sec. 33.

3

American Statecraft in the Founding Generation

GARY J. SCHMITT

If the Declaration of Independence was, as Thomas Jefferson claimed, an "expression of the american mind" at the time of the country's founding, what did it imply about the American approach to statecraft?[1] Little, if courses in American history and civics are taken as a guide. Overwhelmingly, these revolve around the meaning of the Declaration's most famous lines:

> We hold these truths to be self-evident, that all men are created equal, that they are endowed by their Creator with certain unalienable Rights, that among these are Life, Liberty and the pursuit of Happiness.—That to secure these rights, Governments are instituted among Men, deriving their just powers from the consent of the governed.

In such discussions, the Declaration's substance is confined to what constitutes the just grounds and ends for domestic rule and to what extent we have lived up to those precepts as a nation.

But that 55-word snippet from the roughly 1,300-word document had obvious implications broader than America's own political order, even then. It was the first public assertion in human history that a government's legitimacy rested on natural right and not on custom, race, religion, or hereditary claims and that these principles were applicable to all men and all governing regimes. In a world of monarchies and despotisms of various stripes, the Declaration's most famous lines could not help but be seen as a challenge. Writing from Paris, Benjamin Franklin noted, "'Tis a Common Observation here that our Cause is *the Cause of all Mankind*; and that we are fighting for their Liberty in defending our own."[2] (Emphasis in original.)

Given the uncertainty of whether the colonists would prevail in their war of independence against the world's greatest power and whether—should it prevail—a relatively weak and (initially) poorly governed United States would even be able to survive, any challenge that assertion of principle posed might have rightly been seen as distant at best. Nevertheless, as the Declaration's text (in the words of historian David Armitage) "rapidly entered national and international circuits of exchange" and "copies passed from hand to hand, desk to desk, country to country," the claim about what constituted legitimate rule—and the grounds for revolution—could not be ignored completely.[3] As historian Robert Palmer observed,

> The effects of the American Revolution, as a revolution, were imponderable but very great. It inspired a sense of a new era. . . . It gave a whole new dimension to ideas of liberty and equality made familiar by the Enlightenment.[4]

But however the Declaration's assertion of rights was perceived internationally at the time, the document's immediate purpose was more prosaic. To gain assistance from other nations in their war with Great Britain while remaining consonant with international law, the Americans necessarily had to declare that they were a sovereign state and demonstrate their determination to carry on that fight until independence was proven to the world.[5] Accordingly, the Declaration's first paragraph is an assertion that the colonies, having dissolved "the political bands which have connected them" with Britain, are "to assume among the powers of the earth, the separate and equal station to which the Laws of Nature and Nature's God entitle them." Similarly, the Declaration's final paragraph concludes, "That these United Colonies are . . . Free and Independent States" and, as such, "have full Power to levy War, conclude Peace, contract Alliances, establish Commerce, and to do all other Acts and Things which Independent States may of right do." The Declaration was simultaneously setting out the principles that made America unique among the nations of the world and insisting it was a sovereign state like any other.[6]

Even as it did so, the Declaration made clear that revolution in practice was not something to be undertaken lightly—implying that the new American state could be trusted to be a responsible member of the Atlantic order. After announcing the break from Britain, the Declaration then stated that the actual decision to do so was guided by "prudence." Rebellion was not undertaken "for light and transient causes"; rather, it was justified by the British sovereign's "long train of abuses and usurpations." By conditioning the right to revolt on the lengthy catalog of the king's misrule, the Declaration's authors indicated there would be no automatic confrontation by the "united States" with regimes that were neither liberal nor republican.[7] Indeed, the Declaration implies that, had the British monarch not acted as he had and had the colonists' rights not been repeatedly violated, kingly rule would have remained a legitimate form of rule. In short, the Declaration makes no universal call to arms—unlike the later French and Russian Revolutions.

And yet, although the Declaration of Independence does not stipulate a specific form of government to ensure rights, the principles of equality and consent strongly lean in the direction of republican government. Likewise, while the Declaration's tone indicates it is up to each people to vindicate their own rights when threatened, the founding generation could not have failed to recognize that the spread of liberalism would be beneficial to creating an environment in which Americans' rights were better secured and exercised.

In sum, as the country's founding state document, the Declaration presents a set of principles that are potentially expansive—indeed revolutionary—but in a manner that is quite conservative in their application. The new nation carried forward this outlook throughout its earliest decades.

The circumstances in which the Americans found themselves also dictated such a stance. The United States was a weak state in a sea of powerful, non-liberal regimes. The first order of business was survival. Second was the adoption of the policies and institutional tools that would make the rights spelled out in the Declaration more secure.

But once the country was stronger and freed of necessity, what would American statecraft look like? What role, if any, would the country's founding liberalism play in how it conducted its relations with other states?

The Model Treaty

The complex character of American statecraft in the immediate period following the country's founding was captured by the Continental Congress's formal adoption of the so-called Model Treaty on September 17, 1776—a template intended to guide America's relations with other states.[8] Above all else, the Model Treaty focused on bilateral, commercial ties between the United States and other nations. It eschewed formal military or political relations. And it said nothing about preferring ties to or discriminating against different kinds of polities. By treating other states as equals and being treated as an equal in return, Congress hoped, the United States could avoid being drawn into the ever-shifting competition among Europe's great powers.

While undeniably the diplomacy of a weak and ideologically isolated state, the Model Treaty was not simply that. The emphasis on opening freer trade with other nations was consistent with the Americans' own commercial inclinations and their interest in breaking down the mercantilist approach of much of Europe and circumventing (to the extent possible) Britain's domination of international trade through its hegemony over the seas.[9] Writing to Congress from Paris in 1780, John Adams quoted favorably from a monograph about the potentially reforming impact of the American approach to trade:

> N. America is a new primary Planet, which taking its Course in its own orbit, must have an Effect upon the orbit of every other. . . .

... She is mistress of her own fortune, knows that she is so, and will manage that Power which she feels herself possessed of, to establish her own System and change that of Europe.[10]

Informed by Enlightenment thinkers, the American interest in free trade had, if only furtively, a broader goal in mind. Americans were aware of Montesquieu's argument that freer trade would gradually promote more peaceful relations among trading states as their interdependence increased.[11] Additionally, freer trade would increase a nation's commerce and, in turn, expand its prosperity domestically. Greater prosperity, distributed more equally among the population, ideally would generate pressure for greater liberalization within states.[12] By promoting a liberalized trading order, Americans would be putting their own "pursuit of Happiness" on firmer ground while potentially furthering a process leading to more liberal-leaning regimes. The similarity in polities would, as Adams wrote about prospects of a treaty with the Dutch Republic, make ties "natural" and connections "easy."[13]

Dire Straits

The Model Treaty's strategic vision was undercut by the reality that the monarchies and imperialist states then dominating the globe were far from "natural" partners for the United States.[14] According to American diplomats abroad, the new nation had to operate in a world in which the existing powers "watch us with a jealous eye, while we adhere to and flourish under systems diametrically opposite to those which support their governments."[15] Imperial powers maintained a mercantilist approach, keeping exclusive trading privileges within their colonial possessions. More broadly, European countries' international affairs rested on a balance-of-powers approach adopted under the Peace of Westphalia in 1648, which prioritized national sovereignty over questions of religious confession.

With no real power to leverage or impose its will, the United States could not at that point expect its reform program of liberalized trade and expansive neutrality rights to be an effective basis for statecraft. To survive, the United States would need to play its weak hand as best it could within the existing geopolitical order.

The Congress's immediate goal was to gain assistance from France—the one European power with both the resources to provide that assistance and the desire to enact revenge on Britain for its losses in the Seven Years' War. Relying on the framework of the Model Treaty, the Congress sought that help by offering France favored trading status, without more formal political or military ties. Adams, the Model Treaty's principal author, believed the economic benefits that a liberal trade agreement with the United States would generate for France would be sufficient inducement for the French king and his government to offer significant assistance to the American cause without more formal ties.[16] This belief proved to be overoptimistic, as the French price for assistance was a commercial accord along with a mutual defense agreement. Still, the Americans were not averse to adapting their plans to the situation at hand. While they continued to push a diplomatic agenda abroad that avoided political ties based on the Model Treaty, they were aware of the need to bend to necessity.[17]

With the 1783 Treaty of Paris, the United States secured formal peace with Great Britain and London's recognition of the United States as an independent state with borders encompassing all former British lands east of the Mississippi River, north of Florida, and south of Canada. With other provisions covering fishing rights in the Grand Banks and arrangements satisfying outstanding debts and property disputes between the two countries, the Treaty of Paris was, all in all, favorable for the United States.

But those favorable terms did not bring a respite from America's difficult strategic situation. In the north, west, and south, the United States was bounded by Spain and Britain—two imperial powers that had no interest in seeing the young republic prosper. Although France technically remained an ally, its greater fealty was to Spain, and Spain was focused on retaining its North American territories of Louisiana and the Floridas. Moreover, in the absence of alternative overseas markets of any significance, American commerce was still highly dependent on trade with Great Britain—a point of leverage for London that prevented the United States from retaliating against Britain's mercantilist measures.

Britain exposed America's impotence most seriously by refusing to vacate a series of forts it had held in the Northwest Territory now belonging to the United States under the terms of the 1783 treaty. When the United States demanded British forces pull back, the British countered by (correctly) saying the Americans had failed to fulfill their own treaty pledges. With only a small standing force and no federal enforcement capacity to make citizens in states abide by the terms of the treaty, the American government was powerless to remove the British military from United States territory. Similarly, when Spain closed access to the Gulf of Mexico for American trade using the Mississippi River, American diplomats could complain but had no capacity to make Madrid reverse that decision.

Equally as problematic, Spain and Great Britain had allies among the Native American nations that had a mutual interest in preventing Americans from moving deeper into the continent. Absent a rightsized force to police the frontier, Americans moving southwest, west, and northwest could not count on protection from tribal attacks. Abroad, Barbary powers captured ships and enslaved the sailors of American merchants attempting to ply their trade in the Mediterranean. With no navy to protect merchant ships, all the Americans could do was pay tribute and ransom moneys to the piratical ministates.

Americans' own ambitions exacerbated the country's difficult strategic situation. Even during the colonial period, many in North America envisioned a continental empire. With no natural impediment to the continent's growth in population, vast amounts of natural resources, and the seemingly endless stretch of virgin lands to acquire and make productive, it was a reasonable projection of the future. Once the United States had secured from Britain the territories over the Appalachian Mountains, there was little stopping the push to the Mississippi. Guided by the spirit of the Lockean precept that *"As much Land* as a Man Tills, Improves, Cultivates, and can use the Product of, so much is his *Property"* (emphasis in original), the world's largest experiment in "the pursuit of Happiness" was underway.[18]

Nevertheless, if the westward-moving Americans could not be protected from attacks, if they could not bring their products readily to market absent access ports on the Gulf of Mexico, if there was, in short, no effective government to secure their life and property, it was an open question how long they would retain their allegiance to the new government. As George Washington noted in 1784 of those immigrating westward,

> How entirely unconnected with them shall we be, and what troubles may we not apprehend, if the Spaniards on their right, & Gt Britain on the left . . . hold out lures for their trade and alliance. . . .
>
> The Western settlers . . . stand as it were upon a pivot—the touch of a feather, would turn them any way.[19]

Peace, ironically, brought new vulnerabilities, not all of which were a product of hostile states' devising.

To address these vulnerabilities effectively, American statesmen needed better tools and resources. And it was gradually understood that this required a more energetic and more powerful federal government than what the Continental Congress and the Articles of Confederation provided. The "crisis" in governance in the United States in the 1780s was as much about the state of the nation's security as it was about domestic affairs.[20] Reliance on republican martial spirit, Congress as the country's executive, and the states' goodwill to provide for the country's broader needs had proved inadequate during the war and in its aftermath.

Lacking independent taxing power, the federal government was at the states' mercy to fund a military adequate to force the British out of the Northwest Territory, open up the Mississippi, defend settlers from attacks by native tribes, and protect merchant shipping on the high seas and in the Mediterranean. The individual states did none of these. The inability to protect the frontier also meant the price for the government's sale of Western lands was less than it might otherwise have been, reducing further the government's resources. Nor did the federal government have the power to establish a common commercial policy, meaning there was no possibility of an effective, national response to trade restrictions that Britain or other countries imposed on the United States. Finally, Congress had no means to ensure that citizens of the states abided by provisions in the peace treaty intended to satisfy outstanding debts owed to British creditors—a failure in the treaty's execution that the British government used as grounds for refusing to remove its forces from the Northwest Territory. Alexander Hamilton, writing as "Publius" in *Federalist* 15, summarized the situation: "We have neither troops, nor treasury, nor government."[21]

The Federalist Response

The consensus among those attending the Constitutional Convention— implied initially and almost immediately adopted as the working plan— was that the Articles of Confederation had to be replaced. It was essential that a true state with significant powers be erected if the American republic was to survive in a hostile, non-republican world. As Max M. Edling notes in *A Revolution in Favor of Government*,

> In the Constitutional Convention, there was little disagreement about the need to strengthen the military and fiscal powers of the union. Nor was there disagreement about the need to grant Congress the power to regulate commerce and to enforce treaties.[22]

Institutionally, this meant establishing a chief executive sufficiently independent to act with decision, dispatch, and secrecy. It was these qualities, in addition to the possibility of a lengthy tenure in office, that made the president "the most fit agent" to conduct the nation's foreign relations and do so systematically.[23] Additionally, it was important that he be made the unquestioned commander in chief over federal and state (militia) forces when called into service. With an executive so constructed, the government would have someone who could not only deal with immediate emergencies and threats but also take advantage of unforeseen opportunities in the ever-changing constellation of global affairs. Finally, an independent executive with the prospect of a lengthy duration in office could also be incentivized to prepare plans that reached beyond immediate concerns.

In terms of powers, this meant especially giving the new federal Congress authorities in taxes, commerce, and the military that either didn't exist for the Congress of the Confederation or were functionally so circumscribed as to be of little use. Under the new Constitution, Congress would have the unilateral power to tax and borrow money—a power essential for resourcing a professional standing army. There were no limits on how much taxes could be raised, the power to borrow, or the size of the army or navy. The power to tax was essential if the federal government was to reduce its foreign indebtedness and, in turn, establish its creditworthiness abroad. Congress was also given the authority to regulate the country's domestic and foreign commerce—thought necessary to present a unified front in the country's trade relations with mercantilist states.[24]

Most broadly, the federal government's enhanced powers and institutional arrangements were thought necessary to preserve American sovereignty and, with it, the liberties articulated in the Declaration of Independence. By 1787, Americans no longer saw governmental power as the primary threat to liberty but rather the key to sustaining it.[25] The country's most basic concern, its "safety and welfare," required a union that was less likely to give offense to other powers by its failure to abide by its agreements but that maintained sufficient strength to deter those same powers—since the latter would not be indifferent to the United States' "advancement" in power.[26] Compounding the difficulty was the fact that the nation had potential adversaries in Spain and Great Britain in its immediate vicinity. Similarly, because of progress "in the art of navigation," there was less reason to be sanguine about the advantages of having an ocean between America and Europe.[27]

Furthermore, the unrestricted powers given to the Union were appropriate because, the Constitution's advocates argued, it was impossible for a government to know or predict the scale and variety of threats that could arise.[28] True safety, and with it American liberties and prosperity, meant being ahead of the curve on security matters.[29] To resource such a posture and deal with an actual contingency of some unknown scale, it was incumbent that the government have the authority to tax as needed. A dependable revenue stream would allow the government to service the country's debt, maintain the government's credit, and, in turn, borrow as much money as required in a crisis. No major conflict could be resourced sufficiently without loans. Creditworthiness was not only a matter of a nation's reputation but also key to underpinning the nation's security. The Constitution's architects thought these powers, combined with an energetic, independent executive, were necessary to address immediate threats, as well as those on the horizon.

These new capacities were understood to preserve more than just life and liberty. With no limit on reeligibility, presidents might develop and undertake plans to expand what Jefferson would call the "empire of liberty." Combined with the country's expected growth in economic power and population, the government's new tools could, it was imagined, even give the United States the future ability "to dictate the terms of the connection between the old and new world." Defenders of the new constitution were thinking big and long term—"one great American system."[30]

The immediate benefits were substantial. The newly empowered executive could move quickly and decisively with the Neutrality Proclamation to keep the United States out of the conflicts stemming from the French Revolution. He could also oversee foreign relations and conclude a treaty with the British government. While the Jay Treaty was not widely popular, it stabilized commercial relations with Great Britain and resulted in London finally pulling its troops out of the Northwest Territory. And with new powers in hand, Congress, following the treasury secretary's plan, assumed the country's debt, established a national bank, and created the basis for an American financial system that jump-started the country's economy.

The Washington administration also signed a treaty with Spain that resulted in Madrid agreeing to open the Mississippi River to trade. Combined with the retreat of British forces and treaties with Native Americans in the northwest and southwest, that treaty enhanced the economic and security conditions for settling America's western territories. Andrew Cayton notes that "in a decade and a half," the government "had transformed trans-Appalachia from a potential source of revenue, disunion, and chaos into a region of genuine revenue, growing external security, and increasing loyalty to the United States of America."[31]

Edling raises the question of just how much of this improved strategic situation "can be credited to the new modeling of the federal government." His answer is that "the evidence suggests that Spain and Britain concluded treaties with the United States"—which, in turn, isolated their former Native American allies—"because they did not wish to see the American republic allied with their enemies. With war raging in Europe, the United States was approaching, at least temporarily, the point Alexander Hamilton had dreamed of in *Federalist* 11, when 'a price would be set not only upon our friendship, but upon our neutrality.'"[32]

A Hercules in the Cradle?

Washington was satisfied with his first administration's successes in improving the security of the United States. Nevertheless, by the end of his second term, he was concerned that sectionalism and the growth of political factions—with the latter opening the door to foreign interference in America's foreign and domestic deliberations—could undo the unity that had brought about those successes. As Washington asserted in his Farewell Address, "your Union ought to be considered as a main prop of your liberty." Union provides "greater strength, greater resource, proportionably greater security from external danger" and, as a result, "less frequent interruption of" the country's "Peace by foreign nations."[33]

Washington's specific advice was to "cherish public credit" as key to having the resources necessary "to prepare for" possible dangers, creating a deterrent that would make it less likely for the nation to spend even more "to repel" attacks. More famously, Washington warned against American citizens adopting "permanent, inveterate antipathies against particular Nations and passionate attachments for others." To do otherwise, to adopt "an habitual hatred, or an habitual fondness" for another nation, would amount to becoming "in some degree a slave." It would undermine the ability to objectively assess what the country's true course should be. Subsequently, Washington laid down that "the great rule of conduct for" the United States "in regard to foreign Nations is in extending our commercial relations to have with them as little *political* connection as possible."[34] (Emphasis in original.)

Washington's guidance in the Farewell Address is not the strategic straitjacket it is often understood to be. Although he undoubtedly wanted his advice to be taken seriously, it's important to contextualize his advice in the particular circumstances the country was facing. A policy of neutrality, in which no formal favoritism was to be shown in the conflict between France and Great Britain, was necessary because the United States could ill afford becoming involved in that clash despite the improvement in the American strategic situation since the Constitution's formal adoption. Despite American gratitude for French support during the Revolution and some sympathy for France's own revolution, revenues from trade with Britain were vital to American government finances, creditworthiness, and economic prospects. The French market was not a realistic substitute to maintain those benefits. More prosaically, the United States had not created a naval fleet or an army of sufficient size to guarantee the country's safety in a war involving the two greatest powers in Europe—despite now possessing the authorities to do so.

Yet prudence is not the same thing as principle. Washington did not rule out any and all political connections.[35] How could he? After all, a political connection with the French had made independence possible. Although Europe's "set of primary interests" had "none or a very remote relation" to America's, he could hardly believe that this would always be the case given the changes he had already witnessed, not to mention America's own ambitions.

Nor was the United States, in Washington's estimation, destined to be the perpetually weak sister on the world stage. "At no distant period," America could—if it maintained "a steady adherence to" his administration's policies—become "a great Nation." Indeed, "the period is not far off," Washington argued, "when we may choose peace or War, as our interest guided by justice shall counsel."[36]

While Washington's Farewell Address was addressed to the whole nation, his principal targets were those who, following Jefferson and James Madison, believed that the country should lean more to the side of supporting France in its war with Britain, given an existing treaty of alliance with the French, France's critical support in America's war for independence, and the view that France's revolution was an echo of America's own. It was a criticism ignited by the president's proclamation stipulating American neutrality in the spring of 1793.

Hamilton, then treasury secretary and writing under the pseudonym "Pacificus," took up the task of defending the administration's policy. His defense is most remembered for the debate it generated with Madison (writing as "Helvidius") over the extent of the president's executive power. But Hamilton's writing was focused largely on explaining why the United States had no obligation to favor France, allowing him to outline his understanding of which precepts ought to guide American statecraft.

Hamilton initiates his argument by noting that the treaty with France was "defensive" in nature. With France having started the war with Austria, Britain, the Netherlands, Prussia, and Spain, the United States was under no obligation to assist the French. Nor did the Americans owe— out of a sense of gratitude for French assistance during the Revolutionary

War—more than what a strict reading of the treaty required. France's help had been driven not by a desire to see the American republican experiment succeed but by a desire to embarrass and weaken its archenemy, Great Britain. Gratitude, Hamilton argues, is a "sentiment" that should not replace the United States government's obligation to consider the consequences of its policies for America's "existing Millions" and its "future generations."[37]

Moreover, America was in no position to help and risked losing far more than what it might expect to gain from assisting France. With treaties of conciliation with Madrid and London not yet concluded, and lacking a navy and army of any significance, the United States could hardly risk being seen as a cobelligerent on France's side. Spain and Britain surrounded the United States in North America; the country had had no capacity to deal with the British Royal Navy on the high seas and, as already noted, had no real substitute for the government revenues generated by trade with England. "Self preservation," Hamilton writes, "is the first duty of a Nation." Laying down a precept that would be echoed in Washington's Farewell Address, Hamilton warns that Americans should be careful "not to over-rate *foreign friendships*" and to be on "guard against *foreign attachments*."[38] (Emphasis in original.)

Hamilton's defense of the administration's position is certainly realistic but not as constraining as it first appears. When Hamilton argues that Americans should not overrate foreign friendships, he does not preclude ties of friendship altogether; rather, he means one should not let such potential ties cloud one's judgment about one's own country's fundamental interests. As Hamilton himself says, his prescriptions are not to be understood as promoting policies "absolutely selfish."[39] Moreover, by emphasizing America's weakness as one reason for the policy adopted, Hamilton raises indirectly the issue of what the policy might be if and when the United States has become comparatively strong. In a situation in which a country has "*much to hope and not much to fear*," there will presumably be greater flexibility in what policies a government adopts.[40]

As part of the argument that French government behavior was "offensive" in nature and, hence, not requiring American support, Hamilton refers to the French government's general declaration in the fall of 1792 that it was willing to use military force to help a population living under a monarchy replace that with a republican government. Quoting from Emmerich de Vattel's *The Law of Nations*—"that it does not belong to any foreign Power to take cognizance of the administration of the *sovereign* of another country, to set himself up as a judge of his Conduct or to oblige him to alter it" (emphasis in original)—Hamilton argues that not only was it the case that France started the war but also that France was now using military force for reasons that violated international law. Accordingly, this was yet another reason for the United States to stand aside from helping the French.[41]

Nevertheless, Hamilton understood that strict adherence to Vattel's rule would have complicated France's assistance to the American revolutionaries whose argument for independence, and hence the right to seek assistance, rested on claims about the British monarch's maladministration of his colonies. To square the circle as a practical matter—and by doing so stay in harmony with the American attachment to the universal rights found in the Declaration of Independence—Hamilton states that, while governments have no right to issue "a general invitation to insurrection and revolution," it is still "justifiable and meritorious in another nation to afford assistance to the one which has been oppressed & is *in the act* of liberating itself."[42] (Emphasis in original.)

Both Washington and Hamilton offered a realistic assessment of America's early strategic situation and articulated prudent policies to fit it. But neither foreclosed a more ambitious role for the United States in the future. To the contrary, they both foresaw a time when the republic would crawl out of its cradle.

Republican Well-Wishing and More

The most famous statement from the founding generation about the Declaration of Independence and American statecraft is Secretary of State John Quincy Adams's July Fourth address before Congress in 1821. There, Adams famously declares that the United States would not go abroad "in search of monsters to destroy. She is the well-wisher to the freedom and independence of all." But "she is the champion and vindicator only of her own." To act otherwise, Adams argues, would potentially lead the United States down an imperial path in which "she might become dictatress of the world," but "she would be no longer the ruler of her own spirit."[43]

On its face, Adams's prescription is at odds with Hamilton's suggestion that the United States might intervene if an active, liberal rebellion were taking place. However, the restraint Adams prescribes needs to be placed in context as much as Hamilton's and Washington's prescriptions. The indefensible and, ultimately, ineffective colonial rule of Great Britain and the other imperial powers of Europe is the overarching theme of Adams's address. In the case of the United States, distance and the inevitable social bonds of family and local community meant that "long before the Declaration of Independence the great mass of the People of America and of the People of Britain, had become total strangers to each other."[44] Indeed, as Adams privately explained to Edward Everett, the logic of his argument was meant to foreshadow "the downfall of the British Empire in India as an event which must necessarily ensue at no very distant period of time."[45]

Fueling and further justifying this progressive turn in world events, according to Adams, was America's gift to "mankind," the Declaration of Independence.[46] As a state paper announcing independence, it was of no particular consequence, he argued, since throughout history it was not uncommon for one people to break with another. Rather, what was unprecedented was the principle of rights that it set forth: "It was the first solemn declaration by a nation of the only *legitimate* foundation of civil government. It was the corner stone of a new fabric, destined to cover the surface of the globe."[47] (Emphasis in original.) Colonialism was at odds with the principle of consent; thus, it had obvious revolutionary implications for those living under such rule.[48] Noting in a letter shortly thereafter that he had cast prudence aside, Adams ends the address by urging "every individual among the sceptred lords of human kind" to be filled with the revolutionary "spirit" of the Declaration and "go thou, and do likewise."[49]

If the reaction from foreign diplomats and ministers was any indication, the secretary of state's address was hardly received as articulating a model of American restraint. According to the Russian ambassador, it "was a virulent diatribe against England" and a "miserable calumny on the Holy Alliance" of Austria, Prussia, and Russia—an alliance that was asserting the right to reverse by military force liberal turns in European governance. To the Russian diplomat, it was a clear "appeal to the nations of Europe to rise against their Governments."[50]

Despite Adams's claim to have closeted prudence when giving his address, circumstances undoubtedly played a part in what he said. A number of Spain's Latin American colonies were in rebellion, with some already declaring their independence. Sympathy was high in the United States for giving support to the revolutionaries, with the most notable public advocate being Speaker of the House Henry Clay. And, indeed, there was actual American support, which, while not formal, was not insignificant.[51]

This was not surprising. Following the War of 1812, having once again resisted the global power Great Britain, Americans grew more confident about what they believed the republic's place on the world stage to be. Adams's priority in 1821, however, was settling matters with Spain on the North American continent. Having just finalized the Adams–Onís Treaty, in which Spain ceded Florida and its rights to the Pacific Northwest along with settling outstanding issues regarding the boundaries of the Louisiana Purchase, Adams was in no rush to instigate a diplomatic crisis with Madrid. Nonetheless, Adams also believed that Spain was a declining power and would soon lose whatever hold it still had over its Latin American colonies. Rather than retreating from formal recognition of the new states, Adams thought his July Fourth address had implicitly set out "the justice" of their cause and had prepared "for an acknowledgment" of their independence once that was firmly "established."[52]

Eight months later, the Monroe administration announced its intention to recognize the new Latin American republics. As secretary of state, Adams had the task of drafting instructions for the American diplomats assigned to those states. Notably, his instructions came on the heels of the French invasion of Spain—an invasion sanctioned by the Holy Alliance and intended to restore an absolutist monarchy in Spain. The alliance's success in Spain was not something Adams could ignore, as it related to Spain's former colonies, now republics. "The European allies," he wrote, "have viewed the *cause* of the South Americans as rebellion against their lawful sovereign."[53] (Emphasis in original.)

Moreover, there remained a chance of backsliding in these new states, what Adams called a "hankering after monarchy." To meet this, the secretary told one American diplomat that "among the interesting objects of your mission" would be to "promote" liberal constitutionalism.[54] These were "principles of politics and morals" not limited to America but in fact "co-extensive with the surface of the globe."[55] For Adams,

> the emancipation of the South American continent opens up to the whole race of man prospects of futurity, in which this union will be called in the discharge of its duties to itself and to unnumbered ages of posterity to take a conspicuous and leading part.[56]

This was, Adams wrote, a "mighty movement in human affairs," one in which the United States "*may* . . . be called to assume a more active and leading part in its progress."[57] (Emphasis in original.)

With the Monroe Doctrine following six months later—the doctrine warning the European powers not to interfere in the affairs of the Western Hemisphere—Adams might have said that while the United States was still not looking for monsters to destroy, it was no longer in a defensive crouch when it came to supporting liberalism in the Western Hemisphere. In the summer of 1824, Colombia's ambassador to Washington approached the secretary of state about a possible "treaty of alliance" to give the Monroe Doctrine greater specificity in the wake of a possible (if perhaps distant) threat posed by the revisionist powers of the Holy Alliance. In response, Adams said there would be no security treaty. But Adams went on to state that, should those powers ignore the Monroe Doctrine, the president would be ready to go to Congress to adopt measures ensuring that the doctrine would be "efficaciously maintained."[58] While diplomatically worded, the thrust of Adams's reply was that the United States would not stay neutral and would even risk war if the European powers interfered in Colombia's affairs.[59]

In December 1824, the diplomats from Mexico, Colombia, and Central America invited the United States to send representatives to a Pan-American congress in Panama. The conference's goal was to develop measures to increase cooperation among the countries. Adams, now president, told the United States Congress in December 1825 that he had accepted the invitation to the congress, whose intent was to "deliberate upon objects important to the welfare of all."[60] And while Adams made it clear that there would be no treaty making the Monroe Doctrine multilateral, he did intend for the American delegation to push the Latin American states to adopt policies respecting free trade and religious toleration—policies that, if adopted, would affect their domestic governance and reinforce ties with the United States.

Because a proposed agenda for the Pan-American congress included deliberating about possible measures to reduce the transatlantic slave trade and the recognition of the black-led Haitian regime, members of the United States Congress from the slaveholding South were quick to criticize Adams's decision to participate in the Panama conference.[61] Adams argued that the conference would be deliberating about matters "of the highest importance, not only to the future welfare of the whole human race, but bearing directly upon the special interests of this Union," and hence, that it was imperative that the United States be engaged in those deliberations.[62]

Congressional critics maintained that, by agreeing to participate, Adams had put the country on a slippery slope of engagement that ran counter to the long-standing policy of nonentanglement and noninterference as expressed in Washington's Farewell Address.[63] Adams countered that his critics were misreading the address's intent and the specific strategic circumstances that had given rise to it. The nation was no longer weak or "surrounded by European Colonies." Pointing out that nearly 30 years had passed since the address had been written, he argued that "our population, our wealth, our territorial extension, our power, physical and moral, has nearly trebled."[64] Moreover, the advent of republican polities within the Americas (a change Adams described as a "great revolution in human affairs") meant that their policy choices were bound to have "an action and counteraction upon" the United States; it was a reality to which the country "cannot be indifferent."[65] In fine, "reasoning upon this state of things from the sound and judicious principles of Washington, and must we not say, that the period which he predicted as then not far off, has arrived." "Far from conflicting with" Washington's counsel, Adams asserted that the United States' participation in the Panama congress "is directly deducible from, and conformable to it."[66]

An Empire of Liberty

Europe's monarchs were never comfortable with the Declaration of Independence's liberalism. But so long as the United States remained weak, isolated, and committed to neutrality, they had less to fear from those explosive principles. In the wake of cataclysmic wars inspired by the French Revolution, however, absolutist monarchies in Europe could no longer be so sanguine about liberalism's weakness.

And, indeed, absolutist rule would soon be challenged in Italy, Greece, Portugal, and Spain. Under Austria's foreign minister, Prince von Metternich, the Holy Alliance agreed to adopt policies to strengthen their rule domestically and, by 1820, were explicitly asserting the right to intervene militarily against revolutions that threatened other monarchies. This had obvious implications for the former colonial territories, now republics, in Latin America—and potentially for America's strategic interests. With the advent of an explicitly counterrevolutionary program by major European powers, having like-minded states in America's corner of the globe would matter.

The United States would not soon abandon its formal policy of neutrality. But with a firmer sense of its own strength and increased continental security, it was now willing to lean forward to support the principles it had introduced to the world in 1776.

Notes

1. Thomas Jefferson to Henry Lee, May 8, 1825, Founders Online, https://founders.archives.gov/documents/Jefferson/98-01-02-5212.

2. Benjamin Franklin to Samuel Cooper, May 1, 1777, Founders Online, https://founders.archives.gov/documents/Franklin/01-24-02-0004.

3. David Armitage, *The Declaration of Independence: A Global History* (Harvard University Press, 2007), 15. "When word of the Declaration had reached the British colony of Nova Scotia, in August 1776, the British governor allowed only the last paragraph of the document to be printed, lest the rest of it 'gain over to them (the Rebels) many converts, and inflame the minds of his Majesty's loyal and faithful subjects of the Province of *Nova Scotia*.'" (Emphasis in original.) Armitage, *The Declaration of Independence*, 74–75.

4. While, up to this point, the British government had been seen as the most liberal and progressive of existing regimes, the American Revolution "dethroned England, and set up America, as the model for those seeking a better world." R. R. Palmer, *The Age of the Democratic Revolution: A Political History of Europe and America, 1760–1800*, vol. 1, *The Challenge* (Princeton University Press, 1959), 282.

5. Emer de Vattel, "Of Nations or Sovereign States," bk. 1, chap. 1 of *The Law of Nations* (London, 1758). As a matter of record, the Continental Congress passed a resolution of independence on July 2, 1776. Hence, the formal title of the July 4 declaration is not the Declaration of Independence but rather "The Unanimous Declaration of the Thirteen United States of America." The July 4 declaration served to announce to the American public and the world the colonies' break from British rule and the principled reasons justifying it.

6. "Americans did believe they were different, but the purpose of the Declaration was the opposite of isolation. It was to create the legal basis necessary to form alliances

with European powers." Robert Kagan, *Dangerous Nation: America's Place in the World from Its Earliest Days to the Dawn of the Twentieth Century* (Alfred A. Knopf, 2006), 42.

7. Although the Americans declared they were acting prudently in breaking with Great Britain, Europe's monarchs would have rejected the idea that the Americans were living under some crushing despotism or that there was "a [British] design to reduce them under absolute Despotism." However, appearing to follow John Locke's advice from the *Second Treatise of Government* that a people must act "before it is too late, and the evil is past Cure," the Americans could be expected to be ever more vigilant about possible threats from Europe's monarchs. On these points, see C. Bradley Thompson, *America's Revolutionary Mind: A Moral History of the American Revolution and the Declaration That Defined It* (Encounter Books, 2019), 319; and Nathan Tarcov, "Principle and Prudence in Foreign Policy: The Founders' Perspective," *The Public Interest*, Summer 1984, 53, https://nationalaffairs.com/public_interest/detail/principle-and-prudence-in-foreign-policy-the-founders-perspective. Thompson also notes the frequency of the colonists invoking "the famous Latin dictum *obsta principiis* (to nip in the bud, or to resist the beginnings), which they attributed to Machiavelli's *Discourses on Livy.*" Thompson, *America's Revolutionary Mind*, 324.

8. Formally the Plan of Treaties, the template was directly connected to the motion in the Continental Congress to prepare a declaration of independence, with a resolution the following day (June 11) to create a committee "to prepare a plan of treaties to be proposed to foreign powers." Worthington Chauncey Ford, ed., *Journals of the Continental Congress, 1774–1789*, vol. 5, *1776: June 5–October 8* (Government Printing Office, 1906), 431. On June 12, Adams, John Dickinson, Franklin, Benjamin Harrison, and Robert Morris were appointed to that committee, with Adams taking the lead in the plan's actual drafting. The plan was reported to Congress on July 18 and finally voted on, with no major changes, two months later.

9. "By challenging Britain's mercantilist regime, the Americans appeared not only to serve their own interests, but also those of prospective trading partners and of the trading world generally." Peter Onuf and Nicholas Onuf, *Federal Union, Modern World: The Law of Nations in an Age of Revolutions, 1776–1814* (Madison House, 1993), 19. The possibility of free trade providing America a uniquely safe strategic harbor is raised by Thomas Paine in his *Common Sense*: America's "plan is commerce, and that, well attended to, will secure us the peace and friendship of all Europe; because it is the interest of all Europe to have America a free port." *The Writings of Thomas Paine*, ed. Moncure Daniel Conway, vol. 1, *1774–1779* (New York, 1894), 88.

10. John Adams to the President of Congress, April 19, 1780, Founders Online, https://founders.archives.gov/documents/Adams/06-09-02-0115-0002. In this lengthy note to Congress, Adams set about copying and summarizing a pamphlet (*A Memorial to the Sovereigns of Europe, on the Present State of Affairs, Between the Old and New World*) written by Thomas Pownall, a former governor of the Massachusetts Bay Colony. Adams, who was favorably disposed to Pownall for his moderate behavior while governor, wrote one correspondent that the argument set forth in the pamphlet accorded

with the principles that informed his drafting of the Model Treaty. John Adams to Edmund Jenings, July 18, 1780, Founders Online, https://founders.archives.gov/documents/Adams/06-10-02-0005.

11. "The natural effect of commerce is to bring peace. Two nations that negotiate together render themselves mutually dependent." *Montesquieu's "The Spirit of the Laws": A Critical Edition,* trans. W. B. Allen (Anthem Press, 2024), bk. 10, chap. 2. Thomas Paine advocated free trade because of its reforming social prospects as well. See Yuval Levin, *The Great Debate: Edmund Burke, Thomas Paine, and the Birth of Right and Left* (Basic Books, 2014), 118. In *Federalist* 6, Hamilton appears to take a contrary view, listing historical examples of commercially inclined polities engaging in conflicts with neighboring states: "Has commerce hitherto done anything more than change the objects of war?" However, Hamilton concludes his analysis by implying that the Union, empowered to regulate trade and commerce—creating in effect a free trade zone among the states—will eliminate the incentive for conflict among states. *Federalist,* no. 6 (Alexander Hamilton).

12. See Adams to the President of Congress.

13. John Adams, "A Memorial to Their High Mightinesses, the States General of the United Provinces of the Low Countries," April 19, 1781, Founders Online, https://founders.archives.gov/documents/Adams/06-11-02-0204.

14. As John Quincy Adams would later note while serving as secretary of state, although such liberal commerce was "altogether congenial to the spirit of our institutions, . . . the main obstacle to its adoption consists in this: that the fairness of its operation depends upon its being admitted universally." John Quincy Adams to Richard C. Anderson, May 27, 1823, in *Writings of John Quincy Adams,* ed. Worthington Chauncey Ford, vol. 7, 1820–1823 (Greenwood Press, 1968), 461.

15. William S. Smith to John Jay, December 6, 1785, in *The Diplomatic Correspondence of the United States of America from the Treaty of Peace to the Adoption of the Present Constitution* (Washington, DC, 1837), 5:389.

16. Gerald Stourzh, *Benjamin Franklin and American Foreign Policy* (University of Chicago Press, 1954), 126.

17. As Robert Kagan notes, the Americans, such as John Jay and Franklin, were not naive about Europe: "Americans understood the intricacies of the European balance of power, and how to exploit it to their advantage. As colonists they had played on British fears and jealousies of France to further their own expansionist ambitions. As rebels they played on the French desires for revenge. Manipulating European rivalries was the subject of open discussion in the Continental Congress." Kagan, *Dangerous Nation,* 59.

18. John Locke, "Of Property," chap. 2 in *Second Treatise* (London, 1689), § 32, https://press-pubs.uchicago.edu/founders/documents/v1ch16s3.html.

19. George Washington to Benjamin Harrison, October 10, 1784, Founders Online, https://founders.archives.gov/documents/Washington/04-02-02-0082.

20. The key domestic issue as set out in Madison's *Federalist* 10 is how the public good and minority rights were to be secured in a system of majority rule. From that

starting point, Madison spells out the advantages associated with an extended republic, as well as the separation of powers, checks and balances, and the division between federal and state authorities. Given the role those arrangements continue to play in American governance, it is little surprise that it remains the analytic focus of so much commentary on the logic behind the Constitution's creation. As a result, more often ignored is the new constitution's expected contribution to the country's security. For example, when describing the "principal purposes" behind the effort to strengthen the Union under the new constitution, Hamilton lists more items associated with foreign and defense policies than domestic ones: promoting a "common defense," repelling "external attacks," establishing "commerce with other nations," and superintending relations "with foreign countries." In contrast, strengthening the Union is said to be relevant domestically for countering "internal convulsions" and regulating commerce "between the States." *Federalist*, no. 23 (Alexander Hamilton).

21. *Federalist*, no. 15 (Alexander Hamilton).

22. Max M. Edling, *A Revolution in Favor of Government: Origins of the U.S. Constitution and the Making of the American State* (Oxford University Press, 2003), 73.

23. *Federalist*, no. 75 (Alexander Hamilton).

24. As Madison argued at the Virginia Ratification Convention, "The imbecility of our Government enables" other nations "to derive many advantages from our trade, without granting us any return." John P. Kaminski et al., eds., *The Documentary History of the Ratification of the Constitution*, vol. 9, *Ratification of the Constitution by the States: Virginia* (State Historical Society of Wisconsin, 1990), 1034.

25. See, for example, *Virginia Independent Chronicle*, "State Soldier," February 6, 1788, quoted in Herbert J. Storing, "The 'Other' Federalist Papers: A Preliminary Sketch," *The Political Science Reviewer* 6 (Fall 1976): 226.

26. *Federalist*, no. 1 (Alexander Hamilton); and *Federalist*, no. 4 (John Jay).

27. *Federalist*, no. 24 (Alexander Hamilton).

28. *Federalist*, no. 23 (Hamilton).

29. See note 7. As Hamilton said at the Constitutional Convention, "No Governmt. could give us tranquility & happiness at home, which did not possess sufficient stability and strength to make us respectable abroad." Max Farrand, ed., *The Records of the Federal Convention of 1787* (Yale University Press, 1911), 1:467.

30. *Federalist*, no. 11 (Alexander Hamilton).

31. Andrew R. L. Cayton, "Radicals in the 'Western World': The Federalist Conquest of Trans-Appalachian North America," in *Federalists Reconsidered*, ed. Doran Ben-Atar and Barbara B. Oberg (University Press of Virginia, 1998), 95–96.

32. Edling, *A Revolution in Favor of Government*, 131.

33. George Washington, "Farewell Address," September 19, 1796, Founders Online, https://founders.archives.gov/documents/Washington/05-20-02-0440-0002.

34. Washington, "Farewell Address."

35. "Taking care always to keep ourselves, by suitable establishments, on a respectably defensive posture, we may safely trust to temporary alliances for extraordinary emergencies." Washington, "Farewell Address."

36. Washington, "Farewell Address."

37. Alexander Hamilton, "Pacificus No. IV," July 10, 1793, Founders Online, https://founders.archives.gov/documents/Hamilton/01-15-02-0066#ARHN-01-15-02-0066-fn-0001.

38. Alexander Hamilton, "Pacificus No. III," July 6, 1793, Founders Online, https://founders.archives.gov/documents/Hamilton/01-15-02-0055; and Alexander Hamilton, "Pacificus No. VI," July 17, 1793, Founders Online, https://founders.archives.gov/documents/Hamilton/01-15-02-0081.

39. Hamilton, "Pacificus No. IV."

40. Hamilton, "Pacificus No. VI."

41. Alexander Hamilton, "Pacificus No. II," July 3, 1793, Founders Online, https://founders.archives.gov/documents/Hamilton/01-15-02-0050.

42. Hamilton, "Pacificus No. II."

43. John Quincy Adams, *An Address Delivered at the Request of a Committee of the Citizens of Washington; on the Occasion of Reading the Declaration of Independence on the Fourth of July, 1821* (Washington, DC, 1821), 29, https://archive.org/details/addressdelivered1821adam/mode/2up.

44. Adams, *Address*, 14–15.

45. John Quincy Adams to Edward Everett, January 31, 1822, in Ford, *Writings of John Quincy Adams*, 7:197–201.

46. Adams, *Address*, 28.

47. Adams, *Address*, 21.

48. Writing his father in 1816 from London, Adams claims the royalist animosity toward the United States was due to the fact that they thought the United States and not revolutionary France was the "primary" cause for the "propagation of those political principles" that had been the "earthquake" shaking the foundations of European monarchies. See Charles N. Edel, *Nation Builder: John Quincy Adams and the Grand Strategy of the Republic* (Harvard University Press, 2014), 125.

49. Adams, *Address*, 12, 31. Adams noted in a letter shortly thereafter that he had cast prudence aside; on "asking" prudence "to step into the next door, while I should be holding a talk with my countrymen," see John Quincy Adams to Charles Jared Ingersoll, July 23, 1821, in Ford, *Writings of John Quincy Adams*, 7:120.

50. New, more liberal constitutional orders had been established in Naples, Portugal, and Spain in 1820 and in Sardinia in 1821. At the Congress of Troppau, in late fall of 1820, Austria, Prussia, and Russia issued a protocol declaring that such revolutions were threats to other powers and that they could either by peaceful means or by force of arms reverse those changes and bring those states back "into the bosom of the Great Alliance." See Samuel Flagg Bemis, *John Quincy Adams and the Foundations of American Foreign Policy* (Alfred A. Knopf, 1956), 355–59.

51. Although the United States government maintained a formal policy of neutrality, the Madison administration allowed rebel ships in American ports. Privateers, outfitted and operating out of American ports, were free to prey on Spanish vessels.

In addition, "a thriving underground trade network, centered in Philadelphia and Baltimore, supplied the rebel movements with arms, supplies, and, in some cases, mercenary forces." William Earl Weeks, *John Quincy Adams and American Global Empire* (University Press of Kentucky, 1992), 86.

52. Adams to Everett.

53. John Quincy Adams to Richard C. Anderson, May 27, 1823, in Ford, *Writings of John Quincy Adams*, 7:452.

54. John Quincy Adams to Caesar A. Rodney, May 17, 1823, in Ford, *Writings of John Quincy Adams*, 7:426–27.

55. Adams to Anderson, 7:486.

56. Adams to Anderson, 7:486.

57. Adams to Anderson, 7:471.

58. Quoted in Charles Wilson Hackett, "The Development of John Quincy Adams's Policy with Respect to an American Confederation and the Panama Congress, 1822–1825," *The Hispanic American Historical Review* 8, no. 4 (1928): 508–10, https://www.jstor.org/stable/2506393. As is often noted, the Monroe Doctrine's issuance was made possible because it was assumed British naval power would prevent European interference in Latin America. That's undoubtedly true. But Adams's note to the Colombian diplomat indicates that the United States was prepared to assist in case it wasn't.

59. Earlier, in 1823, British Foreign Minister George Canning had suggested a joint Anglo-American declaration forbidding any European attempts at colonization in Latin America. While Adams was concerned that this might eventuate in the United States getting drawn into British affairs in Europe, James Monroe and former Presidents Jefferson and Madison were inclined to pursue the offer of de facto alliance with London with respect to Latin America. Writing to Jefferson, Madison argued, "With the British power & navy combined with our own we have to fear from the rest of the world: and in the great struggle of the Epoch between liberty and despotism, we owe it to ourselves to sustain the former in this hemisphere at least." James Madison to Thomas Jefferson, November 1, 1823, Founders Online, https://founders.archives.gov/documents/Madison/04-03-02-0162.

60. John Quincy Adams, "First Annual Message," December 6, 1825, University of California, Santa Barbara, American Presidency Project, https://www.presidency.ucsb.edu/documents/first-annual-message-2.

61. John Quincy Adams, *Message from the President of the United States* [. . .] (Washington, DC, 1826), 8.

62. Adams, *Message from the President of the United States*, 5.

63. See Senate Committee on Foreign Relations, "Report on Nominations of Richard C. Anderson and John Sergeant to Be Envoys Extraordinary and Ministers Plenipotentiary to the Assembly of the American Nations at Panama," January 16, 1826, in *Compilation of Reports of Committee on Foreign Relations, United States Senate, 1789–1901* (US Government Printing Office, 1901), 4:14.

64. Adams, *Message from the President of the United States*, 10–11.

65. Adams, *Message from the President of the United States*, 3, 11.

66. Adams, *Message from the President of the United States*, 11. See Edel, *Nation Builder*, 213–18.

4

An International Revolution
from the Beginning

LINDSAY M. CHERVINSKY

The sun was just beginning to rise and flicker through the bare trees that encircled the town square and flanked the road to Boston. A soft thudding gradually grew louder, announcing the imminent appearance of new arrivals and drawing outside the group of men who had gathered in the middle of the night at Buckman Tavern. They organized themselves into orderly lines on the common and watched as a single British officer rode forward on horseback. He ordered the men: "Lay down your arms, you damned rebels!"[1]

In a raspy voice wracked by tuberculosis, Captain John Parker ordered his men to go home. Those closest to him heard the orders and turned to leave, but his voice was drowned out by the movement and confusion. A shot rang out from somewhere beyond the town square. There was a tense moment of silence before the morning air was shattered by rounds of volleys.

It was April 19, 1775, and the Revolutionary War had begun. The lone shot by an unknown gunman was later dubbed the "shot heard round the world." If the Massachusetts rebels had been captured and the war immediately suppressed, few history books would mention this small skirmish. Instead, the deaths of eight militiamen and the retreat of British forces to Boston sparked a war that spanned eight years, covered the globe, entangled the most powerful empires and their colonial holdings, and permanently reshaped the international community.

As the United States gears up to celebrate and squabble over the meaning of the 250th anniversary—of the American Revolution, the Army, and the Declaration of Independence—the commemorative celebrations are a reminder that the nation has never been an island unto itself. The Revolution was an international event from the beginning.

Submitted to a Candid World

Historians have debated the origins of the Revolution since David Ramsay published the first history of the United States in 1789.[2] Most nod to the Enlightenment ideals that proclaimed liberty and the natural rights of man. Political conflict over representation in Parliament and the right of taxation certainly played a role. Social conditions, including the colonies' booming population, exacerbated existing tensions. Every historian and every argument agrees, however, that Americans' participation in the global community was at the core of the disagreements that led to the American Revolution.

Eighteenth-century colonists were no strangers to war. Many of the colonies had fought a series of wars against Native nations, but they were largely regional. The Seven Years' War (1756–63) altered the political, social, and economic character of the North American colonies. For the first time, the colonies fought together in the same major conflict. Soldiers from Massachusetts to South Carolina volunteered alongside British regulars to fight the French and their Native allies. The colonies raised money to pay for regiments, food, and armaments. They were immensely proud of their contributions and saw themselves as some of the most patriotic members of the British Empire.

To the victor went the spoils. Under the terms of the 1763 Treaty of Paris, British territory doubled in size, bringing expanded borders to defend, Native peoples to subdue, and land that sorely tempted the colonists. The British government stationed regiments of British regulars on North American territory for the first time to protect these new holdings. They also passed revenue measures to pay down the enormous war debt and support the expanded military, including taxes on luxury items like tea and sugar.

Colonists objected to the revenue measures in principle and practice. They argued that they had already contributed more than their fair share to the war effort. They had spent blood and treasure fighting the French. They had defended their homes from the threat, while Britons at home were far from the gunfire and bloodshed.

In practice, they also resented that the taxes were designed to limit their economic choices. The Sugar Act of 1764 increased taxes on sugar and molasses imported from French and Dutch merchants and called for strict enforcement against smugglers. The bill was designed to force colonists to buy sugar from the British Caribbean islands. Similarly, in 1773, the Tea Act actually lowered prices on tea imported from the East India Company, a British company, to undercut smuggling. Many American merchants enjoyed a tidy profit from these smuggling activities and resented the attack on their livelihood.

American protests against these measures insisted that the colonies could not be taxed without their own political participation. But they also reflected a widespread desire to participate in the global economic market free from imperial limitations. When these protests failed to produce the required political reform, the colonies declared independence.

The famed Declaration of Independence, published in 1776, was an afterthought domestically. The war had begun 15 months earlier. Congress had created the Continental Army, appointed George Washington as commander in chief, and authorized ongoing fighting. In April 1776, the British forces retreated from Boston, licked their wounds in Nova Scotia, and departed for New York City. The world's largest navy arrived in New York Harbor on June 29, 1776.

While the war raged, at least 90 states and localities had already issued their own declarations of independence between April and July of 1776, including Maryland, New Jersey, Rhode Island, and Virginia.[3] The Pennsylvania state legislature declared

> that as the former Legislative powers of this Province cannot
> act without being under oath or affirmations of allegiance to
> the King of Great-Britain, and dependent on him, which by
> the cruel and wicked proceedings of that King and Parliament

of Great Britain, more especially by a late Act of Parliament declaring the Colonists Rebels, and cutting them off from the protection of that Crown, the same has become incapable of legislation, and in that respect totally extinct.[4]

The legislature then resolved to create a new government "formed on the authority of the people only."[5] There was no turning back.

Globally, however, the Declaration was critically important, and the drafting committee, led by John Adams, Benjamin Franklin, and Thomas Jefferson, designed the document with an international readership in mind. They wrote the Declaration to convince European nations that the US was indeed an independent nation, its cause was righteous, and American independence was not inherently anti-monarchy. They crafted language to convince the monarchies in France and Spain to support the overthrow of the British monarchy while trying to reassure them that the same revolutionary forces would not spread to their territories.

The Declaration styled the colonists' rebellion as just by arguing that "Governments are instituted among Men, deriving their just powers from the consent of the governed," to protect mankind's unalienable rights of "Life, Liberty and the pursuit of Happiness." If the "Government becomes destructive of these ends, it is the Right of the People to alter or to abolish it, and to institute new Government."

The document acknowledged that revolution should be a last resort: "Prudence, indeed, will dictate that Governments long established should not be changed for light and transient causes." Extraordinary measures were justified when "a long train of abuses and usurpations" were heaped upon a people with a "design to reduce them under absolute Despotism." In this scenario, and only in this scenario, the people have a duty "to throw off such Government."

The Declaration then listed 27 complaints against King George III as evidence of "repeated injuries and usurpations, all having in direct object the establishment of an absolute Tyranny over these States."

The Declaration closed by reassuring other monarchs that colonists had pursued every peaceful measure before turning to violence. "In every stage of these Oppressions We have Petitioned for Redress in the most humble terms: Our repeated Petitions have been answered only by repeated injury." Accordingly, the colonies declared themselves "Free and Independent States," with the "full Power to levy War, conclude Peace, contract Alliances, establish Commerce, and to do all other Acts and Things which Independent States may of right do."

This list of rights enjoyed by independent nations was not random or arbitrary. Congress could have mentioned any number of responsibilities and privileges. Instead, the Declaration centered on international engagement as the purpose and primary focus of an independent and sovereign nation.

Congress's first actions after declaring independence reflected this commitment. On July 18, Massachusetts delegate Adams presented a draft to Congress of a model treaty, which would serve as a template for future commercial treaties. On September 17, 1776, Congress approved the text, formally naming it the Model Treaty.[6] Over the next several years, Congress ratified treaties with France and the Netherlands based on this template.

A few days after approving the Model Treaty, Congress appointed Franklin as a diplomatic agent. In October, he sailed for France, where he attempted to negotiate for arms and money. But financial support would only go so far. The colonies needed allies. They needed France to enter the war, to use its own navy to relieve the pressure on the colonies and open a new front in the conflict to divide British attention. None of these aims were possible unless France recognized the United States as a sovereign nation.

The rights of independent nations listed in the Declaration—war, alliance, and commerce—reveal the new nation's priorities. These rights are foundational foreign policy actions and the basis for full participation in the international community. From the beginning, the US was committed to that role.

Foreign Relations

The Treaty of Paris ended the Revolutionary War on September 3, 1783. Although the US had been operating as a quasi-independent nation for eight years, the treaty made it real. Great Britain recognized American independence and sovereignty for the first time, inviting other nations to do the same. America's allies, including France, Morocco, the Netherlands, and Spain, had offered recognition during the war. After the treaty, Bremen, Denmark-Norway, Hamburg, the Papal States, Prussia, and many others recognized the new nation over the next decade.

Once independence was secured, foreign relations remained the Confederation Congress's top priority. The United States owed foreign nations millions of dollars from the Revolution. Repaying those debts and loans was a basic first step for the US to exist in the global community. No further trade, loans, or treaties would be possible if Americans did not uphold their earliest agreements. If they failed to repay their debts, foreign nations would not take the US seriously. They would ignore American sovereignty and seize American goods and territory in lieu of payment.

European empires were sorely tempted to meddle in American sovereignty and territory anyway. Because the United States had no money, it could not pay an army or navy to protect its trade, people, or newly recognized borders. American settlements in the West and South were particularly vulnerable to incursions and raids by Native nations and their European allies. European agents used nonviolent means to stir up trouble as well. They encouraged dissatisfaction with the US government in Western communities and encouraged disgruntled Americans to break off and rejoin the European fold.

Congress could not afford to ignore the perils that international actors posed or hide behind the safety that the Atlantic Ocean offered. Instead, maintaining peaceful relations with existing allies and avoiding further conflict dominated Congress's attention in the immediate years after peace. These motivations also prompted massive reform that empowered the federal government to better represent the nation on the world's stage.

In May 1787, representatives from 12 states gathered in Philadelphia to reform the Articles of Confederation, the nation's first governing charter. (Rhode Island refused to send delegates.) Quickly, the delegates voted to scrap the articles and start fresh. After four months, the delegates sent a proposed constitution to Congress and the states for ratification.

The Constitution created a much more powerful federal government and vested it with three critical powers. All three were lacking under the Articles of Confederation and critical to international engagement. First, Congress received the power to raise money. Previously, the Confederation Congress could pass tax assessments, and each state was then expected to raise the required funds however it saw fit. Nevertheless, the Confederation Congress had no power to enforce the assessment, and states frequently ignored these requests. The Constitution empowered the new federal Congress to raise money to pay off foreign debts and raise and supply an army and navy to defend American borders, citizens, and trade.

Second, the new Constitution streamlined the process of foreign policy. Under the Articles of Confederation, the 13 states regularly pursued their own diplomacy when Congress proved inept or unwilling. Unsurprisingly, 13 separate foreign policies produced a giant mess. Going forward, Congress would declare war and the president would be the nation's diplomatic chief.

Third, the federal government claimed responsibility for all trade and economic relationships. No longer would each state negotiate its own duties, taxes, and trade arrangements with foreign nations, squabbling to undercut each other.

Notably, the Constitution left most domestic powers to the states. This power-sharing arrangement reflected not only the federal government system but also delegates' commitment to the United States' place in the global community. The federal government's main responsibility would be to look outward, while the states would focus inward. The US was never expected to be isolated, and the framers envisioned a government that could best represent the American people around the world.

Nor did the world expect the United States to remain separate from the global community. Very quickly, the American Revolution shaped the postwar international landscape far beyond its borders. In the following decades, a series of cascading revolutions tore down ancient regimes and built new republics, ushering in the age of the republic.

One month after Washington was inaugurated as the first president of the United States, the Estates General gathered in Paris to address the financial crisis and social upheaval tearing across France. France's expenditures during the American Revolution had left the monarchy in deep debt. King Louis XVI attempted to reform the inefficient and haphazard tax system, but regional legislatures blocked these efforts. A series of poor harvests and social movements espousing liberty and equality spurred further social unrest. On July 14, 1789, mobs stormed the Bastille, an ancient fortress that housed royal arms and ammunition. The mob executed the prison governor, paraded his head around Paris on a pike, and tore down the Bastille stone by stone—a symbolic end to the ancien régime.

Over the next nine years, a series of governments seized power, drafted new constitutions, exacted vengeance, and remade French society. During the most violent period, the Reign of Terror, the revolutionary government executed King Louis XVI and Queen Marie Antoinette, as well as tens of thousands of innocent civilians, without trial.

The French Revolution of the 1790s ended with the rise of Napoleon Bonaparte. The creation of the French Republic and Napoleon's rise reignited the centuries-old hostility between France and Great Britain. This newest conflict, which stretched over 20 years, defined foreign policy in the early American republic.

The war immediately forced the United States to consider its position. This debate, known as the Neutrality Crisis, was the major foreign policy moment in Washington's administration. In 1778, the US had signed a Treaty of Alliance with France, which obligated it to come to France's aid if France was attacked. But the US was in no position to fight a war. The nation was just beginning to recover economically and environmentally from the Revolution. Even if Americans had wanted to fight, the country had no army or navy to engage in battle.

Washington and his cabinet, including Alexander Hamilton and Jefferson, quickly decided to declare neutrality under a technical loophole. The Treaty with France was a defensive one. France's declaration of war on Great Britain negated any need for the US to offer aid. But enforcing that neutrality without violating the Treaty of Paris with Great Britain (1783) and the Treaty of Amity and Commerce with France (1778) proved harder to navigate.

The French had their own interpretation of the Franco-American treaties and expected American support. If the US could not field an army, then French officials expected a warm welcome in American ports. Citizen Edmund Charles Genêt, the new French minister to the United States, arrived in May 1793 and immediately hired and outfitted a fleet of privateers. Privateers are private ships, captained by civilians, that sail under a letter of marque (or license) from a foreign nation. The French privateers captured British vessels, dragged them back to port, sold off the valuables, and armed the ships to become new privateers.

Privateering was a standard part of 18th-century warfare, but privateers' activities were limited in neutral ports. In neutral waters, privateers could buy essentials, including food and supplies, and make necessary repairs. They could not buy armaments or sell off their captures.

Genêt ignored the Washington administration's proclamation and used Philadelphia's port as his own personal privateer factory. This behavior did not go unnoticed by the president, who lived six blocks from the port, or the British minister to the US, who also resided in the city. Secretary of State Jefferson demanded Genêt cease these activities, but to no avail. In August 1793, Washington and the cabinet requested that France recall Genêt. They also wrote a series of rules that defined neutral behavior for domestic and foreign actors.

Later that fall, two important developments followed. First, France granted Washington's request and issued an order to recall Genêt. This decision was a tacit recognition that the United States, as a sovereign nation, had the right to set its own foreign policy and demand respect for that policy by foreign actors on its soil. Second, Congress codified Washington's rules of neutrality. The law governed periods of neutrality until the end of the 19th century. These precedents laid the foundation of American diplomacy, established the president's dominant role in foreign policy, and demonstrated the importance of international engagement to the early republic.

While Washington's administration established foreign policy foundations, American involvement with the world had just begun. As Washington's presidency ended, the European war extended far beyond the Continent and engulfed Americans, whether they wished to participate or not. British and French vessels patrolled the Atlantic and the Caribbean and were eager to capture American vessels, seize the goods for their war efforts, and impress American sailors into their own armies. From merchants in New England to plantation owners in South Carolina, Americans protested the attacks on their goods and national honor.

In response to these provocations, President Adams sent a three-person diplomatic commission to Paris to negotiate a new trade arrangement and obtain reparations for French naval depredations. After arriving in the fall of 1797, the American commission was met with hostility and demands for bribes, loans, and embarrassing apologies to even begin negotiations. When reports of this treatment arrived in the United States, American outrage was swift and ferocious. Over the next several months, Congress authorized a series of defensive measures to prepare for war, including beefing up coastal defenses, creating a naval department, significantly increasing the Army, and passing legislation designed to root out French sympathizers on American soil.

The conflict, known as the Quasi-War, never escalated to full-fledged war, however, and Adams remained convinced that a diplomatic solution was possible. Tapping into his extensive global network of informants, Adams received assurances from the French government that France had seen the error of its ways and was eager to receive American diplomats with the "respect due to the representative of a free, independent, and powerful nation."[7]

Defying the hardline voices in his own party, Adams nominated another peace commission in February 1799. The next fall, William Richardson

Davie, Chief Justice Oliver Ellsworth, and William Vans Murray signed the Treaty of Mortefontaine with the French Republic. France and the United States have been at peace since this treaty—one of the longest lasting alliances in the world.

Eighteenth- and 19th-century Americans paid close attention to these developments. Voters understood that the United States was still relatively small and weak. Its economy depended on the whims and good will of foreign nations. That did not mean, however, that all Americans shared the same views on foreign policy. Instead, domestic politics were shaped by diplomatic ideologies, biases, and preferences.

The first two political parties, the Federalists and the Democratic-Republicans, held diametrically opposed visions for the republic's future. Federalists supported a strong national government that invested in defense, trade, and industry. Their supporters included merchants, bankers, and traders, and they tended to congregate on the Atlantic Seaboard. Democratic-Republicans visualized a nation of yeoman farmers with a smaller federal government that offered limited protection for agricultural trade but distrusted standing armies and moneyed interests. They viewed cities as dens of corruption and sin, and their supporters congregated in the South and West.

Most importantly, however, the two parties differed on foreign policy. Federalists preferred a close relationship with Great Britain, which was the United States' dominant trading partner and possessed the world's largest navy. Democratic-Republicans nurtured an ideological affinity for France as their sister republic and inheritor of the revolutionary tradition. These debates over alliances dominated state and federal elections from 1794 until the Federalist Party's collapse in the 1820s.

Disagreements over foreign policy sparked the beginning of the end of the Federalist Party. The Arch Federalists, the party's more extreme wing, pressured Adams to pursue war with France in 1798. The threat of war was excellent for the Federalist Party's electoral prospects, and the expanded army served as a spoils system for Federalist supporters. Diplomacy would undermine these political opportunities. Nonetheless,

Adams understood that neutrality with France and Great Britain was in the young nation's best interest. When he pursued diplomacy over his party's objections, former allies began to refer to him as an "evil" to be endured.[8] Arch Federalist leaders, including Hamilton and former Secretary of State Timothy Pickering, campaigned against Adams in the 1800 presidential election. The intraparty strife fueled Democratic-Republican victories in local, state, and federal elections that fall. The Federalist Party never recovered.

Partisan divisions were further exacerbated by international developments, including pandemics, revolutions, and the flow of refugees. In 1793, an outbreak of yellow fever dominated coastal ports from Baltimore to New York. Philadelphia was particularly hard-hit, losing 10 percent of its population to the terrifying disease. With no cure or understanding of the cause, responses to the pandemic split along partisan lines. Federalists blamed immigrants for importing the disease from places like New Orleans and the Caribbean. Democratic-Republicans disagreed, arguing that the squalid conditions in port towns produced the virus. They were both right: Mosquitoes bit people who had recently arrived from warmer climates and were carrying the virus; the mosquitoes then proliferated in standing water and cesspools along the wharves.

The parties responded in a similarly divisive manner to the arrival of refugees fleeing rebellions in Europe and the Caribbean. Democratic-Republicans welcomed the arrival of Irish immigrants retreating from the failed rebellion against Great Britain. Irish immigrants were natural allies because they shared similar hostilities to the British and cast their votes for the pro-French Democratic-Republicans.

On the other hand, Federalists took active measures to restrict the Irish community. They feared, with good reason, that some Irish in America were sending funds to support ongoing rebellions in Great Britain. Furthermore, they questioned the Irish community's loyalty in the event of a French invasion. They worried that the Irish would join the Democratic-Republicans and side with France to tear down the republic from within.

While the Democratic-Republicans welcomed Irish immigrants, they exhibited their own xenophobia toward a separate class of refugees. The inspiring revolutionary rhetoric, first shouted on the streets of Boston, published in the Declaration of Independence in Philadelphia, and then proclaimed outside the Bastille in Paris, irrepressibly made its way to the coffee and sugar plantations on the French colony of Saint-Domingue, now Haiti. The Haitian Revolution began when white planters demanded independence from France, citing the Declaration of the Rights of Man and of the Citizen, which the French National Assembly had published in 1789, declaring all men free and equal. These claims were quickly adopted by the enslaved and free black populations. Eager to avoid conflict, the French government granted citizenship to wealthy free black residents. When white planters refused to recognize their citizenship, fighting broke out between the island's white and black residents.

In August 1791, the localized skirmishes exploded into a full-fledged race war, expanding to include an estimated 100,000 enslaved people. By the next year, enslaved rebels controlled one-third of the island. Over the next 12 years, British, French, and Spanish forces attempted to regain control of the island, reestablish slavery, and seize control of the sugar production. Yellow fever and malaria outbreaks decimated the European forces' ranks, and the Haitian forces, led by General Toussaint Louverture, defeated the remaining armies. The last French forces capitulated in 1803, and Haiti declared its independence on January 1, 1804.

Democratic-Republicans were terrified that the refugees fleeing the Haitian Revolution, who often brought enslaved people with them, would import slave uprisings to the South. In October 1800, Gabriel's Rebellion, the largest planned slave revolt at that point in US history, seemed to validate these fears.

The history of the first decades of the United States cannot be separated from global wars, trade, pandemics, social movements, or migration. Nor did 18th-century Americans wish to see themselves as separate. They declared independence to participate fully in the international community and fought for the nation's ability to do so in the future.

A Growing Power

As a country that was still relatively small with limited military muscle, the 19th-century United States largely played the role of spoiler on the world stage. The US was not shaping the global order, but it was scrappy and could still pose plenty of irritation for European empires.

As early as the 1820s, however, Americans began to envision a future in which they would enforce their worldview on other nations. In 1823, Secretary of State John Quincy Adams penned a theory of international engagement, which became known as the Monroe Doctrine. President James Monroe included Adams's language in his presidential address to Congress in December 1823, while Adams asserted the same message in his correspondence with Great Britain and other foreign nations.

The Monroe Doctrine declared the Western Hemisphere closed to European meddling and claimed the hemisphere as the United States' sphere of influence. In 1823, the US had little power to enforce this doctrine.[9] The British and French armies far outnumbered American forces, and the British navy ruled the seas. The Monroe Doctrine survived because the British navy tolerated it.

By the end of the 19th century, the US was poised to put some heft behind the rhetoric. American economic growth and territorial expansion coincided with a mindset shift. No longer were many Americans content to limit their ambitions to the North American continent; they were ready to join the ranks of global empires.

Under President William McKinley, the US fought the Spanish-American War. The American victory effectively ended Spanish presence in the Western Hemisphere. The United States added Guam, the Philippines, and Puerto Rico to its imperial territory and seized Cuba as an American protectorate.

Theodore Roosevelt had enthusiastically participated in the war, leading his cavalry troops, known as the "Rough Riders." They gained fame for their bold charge up Kettle Hill in the Battle of San Juan Hill. Roosevelt cherished his "bully fight" in the "splendid little war,"[10] and he brought this expansionist zeal to his presidency.

Like Monroe 80 years earlier, Roosevelt used his 1904 State of the Union address to make a major foreign policy declaration. He announced that the US had the right and intention to interfere in the affairs of Latin American nations if they committed "chronic wrongdoing," which produced the "loosening of the ties of civilized society."[11]

Roosevelt backed up his words with warships. In the fall of 1903, he sent naval vessels to Panama City to support Panamanian independence from Colombia. In the shadow of American cannons, Panama signed the Hay–Bunau-Varilla Treaty, which ceded control of a 10-mile strip for the Panama Canal. In return, Panama received a onetime $10 million payment and an annual annuity of $250,000. In 1908, Roosevelt personally visited the construction site, which was completed in 1914 and produced the first transisthmian canal.[12]

The two World Wars cemented the United States' role as a global superpower. While it didn't fight the longest, sacrifice the most men, or endure the worst devastation, its participation tipped the scales toward victory. After the wreckage of World War II, the US emerged unparalleled in its fiscal and military might. The United States had served as the Allies' factory, and the fighting had largely taken place far from American shores, leaving the country relatively unscathed compared with the rest of the world.

In the decades after World War II, the Soviet Union gained ground and challenged the Western world in the Cold War. The United States imperfectly led the coalition for democracy against the Soviets and their Communist allies.

In previous generations, the United States' political parties had often squabbled over the appropriate level of foreign engagement and isolation. During the Cold War, the Democratic and Republican Parties united in their view of the Soviets as the nation's primary threat. They differed on how best to combat the Communist menace, but they notably agreed on foreign policy's role. At the beginning of the Cold War, Senator Arthur Vandenberg, chairman of the Senate Foreign Relations Committee, coined the perfect phrase to characterize the era: "Politics stops at the water's edge."[3] That might have been true during the Cold War, but it was not often the case in US history.

In between conflicts, isolationist sentiment often gained traction. In the 1920s, many Americans questioned the futility and senseless loss of life in World War I. In the 1950s, the Republican Party's isolationist wing urged a retrenchment after the expenses of World War II, the rebuilding of the world under the Marshall Plan, and the stalemated war in Korea. The failed "forever wars" in the Middle East, the global economic collapse in 2008, and the lack of accountability for both have produced a resurgence of isolationism in the past two decades.

The Separate and Equal Station

The American Revolution is a reminder that hiding from the world is not, and was never, possible. There are no oceans large enough to keep us isolated from a world characterized by the movement of people, ideas, goods, and contagions. In the 18th century, those oceans took months to cross in small wooden vessels battered by wind and waves. Today, airplanes cross them in a matter of hours. Words and images cover the distance online in nanoseconds.

As we celebrate the Declaration of Independence's 250th anniversary, we should embrace America's role in the world—one that the revolutionaries fought so hard to achieve.

Notes

1. EyeWitnesstoHistory.com, "Battle at Lexington Green, 1775," 2001, http://www.eyewitnesstohistory.com/lexington.htm.

2. David Ramsay, *The History of the American Revolution*, 2 vols. (Philadelphia, 1789).

3. Pauline Maier, *American Scripture: Making the Declaration of Independence* (Vintage Books, 1997), 47–49.

4. Robert McPherson, "In Committee for York County, May 30, 1776," in *Pennsylvania in the War of the Revolution, Associated Battalions and Militia, 1775–1783*, ed. William H. Egle (Harrisburg, PA, 1888), 2:545, https://archive.org/details/pennsylvaniaser214harruoft/pennsylvaniaser214harruoft/page/544/mode/2up.

5. McPherson, "In Committee for York County, May 30, 1776."

6. See US State Department, Office of the Historian, "The Model Treaty, 1776," https://history.state.gov/milestones/1776-1783/model-treaty.

7. William Vans Murray to John Adams, October 7, 1798, Founders Online, https://founders.archives.gov/documents/Adams/99-02-02-3088.

8. Theodore Sedgwick to Alexander Hamilton, February 7, 1799, Founders Online, https://founders.archives.gov/documents/Hamilton/01-22-02-0274.

9. National Archives, "Monroe Doctrine (1823)," https://www.archives.gov/milestone-documents/monroe-doctrine.

10. See Raymond K. Bluhm, "Battle of San Juan Hill," *Britannica*, https://www.britannica.com/event/Battle-of-San-Juan-Hill; and Michael Richman, "A 'Splendid Little War' Built America's Empire," *The Washington Post*, April 7, 1998, https://www.washingtonpost.com/archive/1998/04/08/a-splendid-little-war-built-americas-empire/0cc1f34f-cfdd-4e93-9c1a-85893e25ebdc/.

11. Theodore Roosevelt, "Roosevelt Corollary to the Monroe Doctrine," Teaching American History, December 6, 1904, https://teachingamericanhistory.org/document/roosevelt-corollary-to-monroe-doctrine/.

12. US State Department, Office of the Historian, "Building the Panama Canal, 1903–1914," https://history.state.gov/milestones/1899-1913/panama-canal.

13. US Senate, "Arthur Vandenberg: A Featured Biography," https://www.senate.gov/senators/FeaturedBios/Featured_Bio_Vandenberg.htm.

5

The Revolution and the Birth of
American International Relations

ELIGA H. GOULD

The Declaration of Independence is not long. At just over 1,300 words, the United States' first and most iconic founding document easily fits on a single page. That may be why it is the only document Americans can reliably quote by heart. Yet this familiarity obscures as much as it reveals. The Declaration's best-known phrase—"We hold these truths to be self-evident, that all men are created equal"—appears in the second paragraph, not the first. Even more surprising for many readers is how much space Thomas Jefferson, who wrote the first draft, devoted to the constitutional and legal violations that made George III "unfit to be the ruler of a free people." Those grievances, however, hold the key to the words that Americans in 1776 found hardest to accept and whose larger message can still be difficult to hear. After itemizing the king's 27 abuses and accusing the British people of being equally "deaf to the voice of justice and of consanguinity," the signers pledged to hold the British monarch and his subjects as they did the rest of mankind: "Enemies in War, in Peace Friends."

There was—and is—no question about Congress's commitment to the first part of that chiasmus. In the official copy that John Dunlap printed in his Philadelphia shop on the evening of July 4, the Declaration's grievances occupy the middle 37 lines, or slightly more than half the broadsheet's 66. Some of the king's transgressions resonate today—"imposing Taxes on us without our Consent," for example. Others require explanation. To Americans at the time, all suggested that George III and his subjects had become avowed enemies and could be treated as such. During the lead-up to Congress's momentous vote, one of the main reasons for declaring independence was to make that war easier to prosecute. Not only were Britain's European rivals more likely to form alliances with a union of independent states than with colonies rebelling against their king, but a war for independence meant fighting for "a single simple line," as Thomas Paine argued in *Common Sense*. A civil war for reconciliation with Britain's treacherous government, by contrast, was "*a matter exceedingly perplexed and complicated.*" (Emphasis in original.) It was clear which struggle Americans stood a better chance of winning.[1]

Yet the promise in the couplet's second half also mattered. According to the law of nations, which the Declaration's preamble called the "Laws of Nature and of Nature's God," peace and friendship, not enmity and war, were the ordinary conditions in relations between civilized states. To be accepted as one of the powers of the earth, the former colonies needed to show they had the capacity—as the final paragraph states— "to levy War, conclude Peace, contract Alliances, establish Commerce, and to do all other Acts and Things which Independent States may of right do." Although defeating Britain was the first and most important of those tasks, the only victory that France and Europe's other great powers were likely to support was one that resulted in peace. And making peace with Britain's tyrannical king and the people who served and supported him, as Paine cautioned, would not be easy.

That, however, was Congress's promise. As spelled out in the 1783 peace treaty with Britain and, four years later, in the Constitution, that pledge would require concessions at least as difficult to accept as the war that Americans so boldly embraced. Its legacy remains a challenge to this day.

Peace and Aggression

Despite the obstacles to making peace with Britain, Congress insisted that Americans were a peaceful people. During the summer of 1775, in a proclamation that Jefferson helped write for George Washington to publish once he took command of the army outside Boston, Congress depicted the resort to arms as a move that Americans took reluctantly. Until Parliament claimed new powers with the Sugar and Stamp Acts of 1764 and 1765, relations with the mother country had been "peaceable and respectful." For the past decade, Americans had *"reasoned [and] remonstrated with Parliament in the most mild and decent Language."*[2] (Emphasis in original.)

Americans' boycott of British goods meant even their resistance to the harsh Coercive Acts (1774) and support for the people of Massachusetts were nonviolent. But instead of being treated with moderation, they were subjected to "an unprovoked Assault" on April 19 by General Thomas Gage's soldiers, who murdered eight of their fellow subjects on Lexington Common before marching "in warlike array" on Concord. Although the redcoats were repulsed at the North Bridge, the first colonists to respond in kind were "country people suddenly assembled to repel this cruel aggression." Only when confronted with demands for their "unconditional submission" did Americans choose resistance by force. Even then, their goal was reconciliation and reunion.[3]

The peace that Americans imagined, however, depended on Britain's willingness to make some unconditional submissions of its own. As signaled in a series of letters between 1774 and 1776 to the inhabitants of Quebec, one of Congress's principal war aims was to absorb Canada, Nova Scotia, and the rest of British North America and, in so doing, purge the entire continent of Britain's hostile presence. In making the case for adding Canada to the Union, Congress appealed to a "common liberty" that it claimed Americans shared with the province's 90,000 French habitants.[4] But all three letters warned Canadians that the alternative to joining their southern neighbors was war. "You are a small people, compared to those who with open arms invite you into a fellowship," wrote the authors of the first letter. Which, they asked, was better: "to have all the rest of North-America your unalterable friends, or your inveterate enemies"?[5]

During the fall of 1775, Continental soldiers under Major Generals Richard Montgomery and Benedict Arnold made good on that threat with a two-pronged invasion of the former French colony, capturing Montreal and besieging Quebec City. The campaign turned Montgomery, who lost his life in a New Year's Eve assault on Quebec, into the Revolutionary War's first American national hero and made a lasting impression on the thinking about the Union.[6] In the Articles of Confederation, Congress named Canada as the one British province that could join without the states' prior approval. Canada also appeared along with Britain's other colonies as a prospective state in the Model Treaty, drafted to guide negotiations with France. It remained an invasion target for the rest of the war.[7]

Closely related to these continental ambitions were Congress's unilateral plans for the 150,000 native inhabitants of Indian country. In a series of talks during the summer and fall of 1775, Congress warned the king's Indigenous allies not to become involved in the war with Britain. "This is a family quarrel," Congress's commissioners told the Six Nations of the Haudenosaunee (Iroquois Confederacy) at Onondaga, New York. "You Indians are not concerned in it."[8]

Ultimately, however, the Native Americans faced the same dilemma as the Canadians. In an early draft of the Articles of Confederation, Benjamin Franklin suggested bringing the Six Nations into the Union in a "perpetual Alliance." Another possibility was to make them a state with the right to send representatives to Congress. That was what federal commissioners promised the Delaware Nation in the 1778 Treaty of Fort Pitt.[9] But most Indigenous leaders, who doubted that good would come from either offer, preferred the devil they knew and sided with Britain. Patriots responded by subjecting Native Americans to the same "undistinguished destruction of all ages, sexes and conditions" that the Declaration accused "merciless Indian Savages" of practicing on them. By the war's end, the Haudenosaunees' ancestral homeland in the Mohawk Valley was a desolate landscape of charred farms and villages. Its former inhabitants were either fighting for the king or huddled in refugee camps under the watchful eye of the British garrison at Fort Niagara.[10]

Overall, the largest and most influential group that Congress expected to submit was the Loyalists. Although Patriots hoped (or said they hoped) that gentler means would suffice, the Declaration turned the half million or so Americans who remained loyal to George III—roughly 20 percent of the colonies' prewar white population—into traitors, rebels, and disturbers of the peace.[11] In *The American Crisis*, written while he was retreating with Washington's army across New Jersey in December 1776, Paine placed much of the blame for General William Howe's success on the Tories, as the Loyalists were called. "And what is a Tory?" he asked. The question practically answered itself. "Every Tory," Paine said, "is a coward" whose treachery threatened the new Union's existence. Until recently, revolutionary leaders had been "tender in raising the cry against these men, and used numberless arguments to show them their danger, but it will not do to sacrifice a world either to their folly or their baseness. The period is now arrived," he warned, "in which either they or we must change our sentiments, or one or both must fall."[12]

Such words made the king's adherents legitimate targets for what historian Lisa Ford calls "a peaceable riot" by Patriot crowds in Boston and for the likes of Colonel Charles Lynch of Virginia, whose flogging of suspected Tories is often mentioned as the origin of "lynching" and "lynch law" in the South.[13] States also enforced conformity by statute. Americans who refused to submit to the new state governments were barred from holding office. They were jailed or banished, had their property confiscated, lost the right to practice their profession or craft, and—in extreme cases—were sentenced to death.[14]

By threatening their neighbors and silencing their critics, Congress and the states opened themselves to allegations that they were the ones levying war without just cause, not the king's subjects.[15] In *An Answer to the Declaration of the American Congress*, commissioned by Lord North's ministry during the fall of 1776, the English attorney and pamphleteer John Lind mounted a line-by-line rebuttal of Jefferson's grievances. Starting with the sugar and stamp taxes, there was nothing oppressive or unconstitutional (or new), Lind said, about any of the powers that Britain's king and Parliament stood accused of abusing. If anyone was guilty of unprovoked aggression, it was Congress. In a "Short Review" appended at the back, Lind's friend Jeremy Bentham broadened the pamphlet's critique to include what Bentham decried as the Declaration's hostility to all government. As the rebellious colonists would soon discover, *"there is no peace with them, but the peace of the King; no war with them, but that war, which offended justice wages against criminals."* (Emphasis in original.) In early November, British officials sent 500 copies of the tract to New York, where they hoped it would open Americans' eyes to the error of their ways.[16]

For eight long years, from "the shot heard round the world"[17] at Concord's North Bridge to Congress's cessation of hostilities on April 18, 1783, the back-and-forth over which side really wanted peace and which was using it as a pretext featured prominently in what military historian John Shy called the struggle for the "hearts and minds" of the American people. As suggested by Shy's reference to the Vietnam War, the war on America's Eastern Seaboard and in the Union's most densely populated areas was not one conflict but two.[18]

In the first, the regular war that pitted the Continental Army against British, German, and Irish soldiers, Britain enjoyed substantial advantages, especially before France and Spain entered on America's side. But the war was also an insurgency waged by local militias and armed partisans against civilians. Although the British made effective use of Loyalist paramilitaries in areas they controlled, the advantage in that war lay almost entirely with Congress's supporters. Unless they lived in occupied New York or another British stronghold, Americans with doubts about independence faced a stark choice: Either keep their heads down and their mouths shut or leave. In most places—including where Loyalists were a substantial but cowed minority—peace meant whatever Congress and the new state governments said.

Broken Promises

Such tactics were brutally effective, contributing to General Charles Cornwallis's surrender at Yorktown on October 19, 1781; Lord North's resignation the following spring; and the decision several months later to open peace talks in Paris. British leaders took each of these steps reluctantly, and no one more so than George III. With the king's blessing, Lord Shelburne, whose government negotiated the preliminary articles of peace, spent the summer of 1782 trying to persuade Franklin and his fellow commissioners to accept Britain's acknowledgment of Congress's legislative independence while keeping the former colonies nominally subject to the Crown.[19]

When the provisional treaty with its "unconditional" recognition of the United States reached London, the king was devastated. During his speech to Parliament on December 5, those present noted that when the unhappy monarch came to the words "offer to declare them," he paused. Whether he was "embarrassed," wrote New England merchant Elkanah Watson (who sat next to Admiral Richard Howe during the oration), unable to see his text because of "the darkness of the room, or affected by a very *natural emotion*" was impossible to say. (Emphasis in original.) Whatever the reason, the king stopped, collected himself, and resumed. He had offered, he said in a strained voice, to declare the colonies "*free and independent States*." (Emphasis in original.) The speech ended with an appeal to the Almighty that Americans might avoid the calamities that invariably attended the destruction of monarchical power.[20]

Although the king was forced to yield on American sovereignty, the Treaty of Paris was hardly the unconditional peace that Congress had imagined in 1776. Instead, it came with conditions, all based on the premise that Congress had the power to do the "Acts and Things" that, in the Declaration's words, "Independent States may of right do." Article I recognized the former colonies as "free, sovereign and independent States." The other nine treated the United States as a power in its own right—an empire of liberty, as Americans had begun describing the Union, where responsibility for declaring war and making peace, taking and controlling territory, and ensuring that the treaty was enforced belonged to Congress.[21] Significantly, in the second article, which placed the new nation's western border on the Mississippi River, the cession was to the Union as a whole, with nary a mention of Virginia or the other states with claims to that territory.

The vastness of the domain, obtained despite lack of agreement over whether the title should be vested in Congress, the states, or—as Britain, France, and Spain all urged during the Paris talks—the Indigenous nations to whom the land belonged, was breathtaking. Was the Union a marriage of convenience between 13 self-governing states or a unitary power like the British Empire? The treaty didn't say. Congress, however, was the signatory. The only way for Americans to satisfy their obligations to other governments (and, ultimately, to themselves) was for the states in the first article to accept Congress's authority in the other nine.

But would, or could, Congress meet Britain's conditions for peace? To judge from the response to the treaty's protections for "real British subjects" and Loyalists, the answer was no. The clearest safeguards appeared in Article IV, which pledged that British creditors, including Loyalists, would "meet with no lawful impediment" to the collection of approximately £5 million in American debts contracted before the war, and Article VI, which barred actions against the Loyalists once hostilities had ceased. In Article V, by contrast, the peacemakers conceded the limits on Congress's authority by requiring only that it "earnestly recommend" the states to compensate Loyalists for losses they had sustained.[22]

Having endured tarring and feathering, imprisonment, and the loss of their homes and property, the king's adherents responded by leaving in droves. In many places, Patriots took the preliminary treaty's arrival in Philadelphia on March, 12, 1783, as a chance for new acts of retribution. By late November, when the last British transports left New York, some 60,000 refugees had decamped to Florida, the Bahamas, Jamaica, Canada, and—above all—Nova Scotia. Not until the 20th-century partitions of Ireland, India, and Palestine would the British Empire experience a comparable out-migration. Instead of the pan–North American league of friendship that Congress had imagined in 1776, Americans faced a hostile future on a divided continent.[23]

In Britain, where the Loyalists enjoyed sympathy and support, and ultimately in Parliament, the scale of this diaspora proved two things.

First, Shelburne's concessions to the Americans were much too gener-ous, and second, Congress was incapable of fulfilling its side of the bar-gain. Emboldened by this double betrayal, the successor ministry of Lord North and Charles James Fox, followed in early 1784 by the younger Wil-liam Pitt, proceeded to renege on Britain's treaty obligations. During the spring of 1783, manipulating ambiguities in the armistice signed at Ver-sailles by Britain, France, Spain, and the United States, Admiral Robert Digby, commander of the king's sea forces at New York, struck the first blow. He authorized British cruisers to continue taking "rebel" prizes for a full month after Congress suspended maritime hostilities on March 3.[24]

Meanwhile, Digby's counterpart on land, General Sir Guy Carleton, allowed nearly 3,000 African Americans to depart for Nova Scotia, despite language in Article VII requiring the British to evacuate without "carry-ing away any negroes or other property of the American inhabitants."[25] Although as many as 10 percent were enslaved servants of white Loyalists, most were former bondsmen and women who had self-emancipated by joining the British army in the Carolinas, Georgia, and Virginia. One, a soldier named Harry Washington, had labored before the war as a hostler at Mount Vernon. According to Carleton's secretary, Maurice Morgann, Harry Washington's former master cursed with the "ferocity of a captain of banditti" when he learned what the British intended, but George Wash-ington and Congress could do little.[26]

Along the border with Canada, from the mouth of Lake Champlain to the northern entrances to Lakes Huron and Michigan, Britain committed a second violation of Article VII by refusing to withdraw "with all con-venient speed"[27] from Detroit, Niagara, and seven other strongholds. All were now in American territory and well-placed to help the king's Native American allies foil plans by Congress and eastern speculators to con-fiscate Indian land and turn it into real estate for American settlers.[28] According to Lord Sydney, who issued the order to retain the forts on April 8, 1784, a day before the king ratified the peace treaty, the occupation would continue until American obligations to British creditors and the Loyalists were fulfilled.[29]

In Virginia, whose citizens owed more than £2 million—nearly half the American total—the debtors included both wealthy planters like Jefferson, who were able and mostly willing to pay, and struggling farmers, who were not. Making the grievances of the latter its own, the planter-dominated legislature retaliated in time-honored populist fashion by prohibiting British creditors from suing in state courts until the forts were in American hands. The assembly also made debt recovery contingent on compensation for enslavers whose black "property" had left with Carleton.[30] Neither eventuality seemed likely.

For ordinary Americans—most of whom did not own slaves or have claims in Indian country but who were all, to varying degrees, participants in the Union's export-dependent economy—Britain's final broken promise was the most devastating. During the summer and fall of 1782, Shelburne considered allowing American citizens to resume trading with Britain and its remaining colonies as if they were still British subjects. With the prime minister's support, Richard Oswald, the British peace commissioner, included a pledge in the preliminary articles that the final treaty would "Secure . . . perpetual Peace and Harmony" with a provision for full commercial reciprocity.[31]

For Shelburne's British critics, the most vocal of whom were Loyalists in exile (like Franklin's estranged son, New Jersey Governor William Franklin), granting the former rebels free access to British ports was one concession too many. On July 2, 1783, the Privy Council closed the West Indies to ships from the United States. At a stroke, Americans lost their most important prewar source of hard currency. Although precise measures are difficult, per capita income in parts of the Union plunged by as much as 50 percent—a contraction comparable to the Great Depression.[32] In the eastern seaports, the downturn forced many merchants into bankruptcy, but the wealthy and well-connected were not the only victims. Worcester County, Massachusetts, recorded 2,000 suits for debt in 1784, an astonishing number for a jurisdiction with a total population of 50,000. On the coast, where New England's shipyards had accounted for one-third of Britain's merchant marine before the war, the shipbuilding industry all but collapsed.[33]

Enforcing the Peace

Britain's refusal to fulfill its peace commitments until Americans fulfilled theirs placed Congress in a difficult position. One way to make the treaty's promised benefits a reality was to retaliate forcefully and unilaterally against Britain's subjects and supporters in North America. That was what Congress attempted to do with the Treaty of Fort Stanwix, which federal commissioners concluded in 1784 with the Haudenosaunee Confederacy near the headwaters of the Mohawk River. Mindful of the British garrisons at nearby Oswego and Niagara and of the assistance that the Six Nations were continuing to receive from British Indian agents in Canada, the Union's negotiators insisted that the Haudenosaunees accept they were a conquered people. It was an absurd claim, disregarding both well-established norms of Indian diplomacy and the reversals that Indigenous leaders such as Mohawk War Chief Joseph Brant had inflicted on state and Continental forces during the war.[34]

Claiming native land by right of conquest also greatly exaggerated Congress's ability to impose its will once the war was over.[35] By the time the Northwest Ordinance was enacted in the summer of 1787, Congress had abandoned conquest theory, pledging not to take Indians' land "without their consent." Although the ordinance included an ominous and revealing exception for land seized during "just and lawful wars," negotiation would once again be the way to make peace in Indian country—albeit on terms that invariably favored the Union and with promises that were often broken.[36]

Despite widespread support for retaliatory measures, Congress faced similar obstacles in its efforts to force Britain to lift restrictions on American ships and goods. Because it lacked the authority under the Articles of Confederation to tax or regulate commerce, the most Congress and Secretary of Foreign Affairs John Jay could do was encourage states to take the lead. In New England and the mid-Atlantic, one unintended consequence was a growing demand for protective tariffs to shield nascent industries from foreign, usually British, competition.[37] In terms of pressuring Britain to change its trade laws, however, the policy failed. Although most states complied, the result was a patchwork of laws and regulations that British merchants and shipowners proved adept at avoiding, often with help from American associates.

For "nationalists"—as supporters of a stronger Union in Congress and the press were known—the need for a unified strategy against Britain became one of the principal arguments for constitutional reform.[38] Among the earliest and most forceful advocates was Paine. "While we have no national system of commerce," Paine warned readers of his final essay in The American Crisis (1783), the former colonies would remain subject to Britain's "laws and proclamations." When the states acted as one, the American Union was formidable; "separated, she [was] a medley of individual nothings."[39]

Congress did make some headway in persuading the states to protect the rights of British creditors and repeal anti-Tory laws. The first victory occurred in New York, where a brewery leased by the British army to Joshua Waddington and Evelyn Pierrepont burned to the ground on November 25, 1783, days before the city's evacuation. Ordinarily, the rules of war forgave wartime injuries by occupying armies. Under New York's anti-Tory Trespass Act, however, residents who left "by reason of the invasion of the enemy" could bring actions for punitive damages against anyone who occupied, injured, or destroyed their property in their absence.[40] Because Britain's occupation was illegal, the law barred defenses based on military orders.

In early 1784, Elizabeth Rutgers, the brewery's widowed owner, sued the two British merchants for £8,000. Appearing for the defense, Alexander Hamilton argued that the Trespass Act violated the law of nations, the peace treaty with Britain, and Congress's authority under the Articles of Confederation. The war's "justness or injustice," Hamilton said, was irrelevant. Although the judge declined to overturn the law, he ruled that repealing the law of nations "could not have been" the legislature's intention. Because Waddington and Pierrepont initially held the brewery from Britain's civilian commissary, they were liable for damages between 1778 and 1780, but once the army assumed the license, their liability ceased.

The jury awarded Rutgers less than a tenth of what she had sought.[41]

Meanwhile, with the notable exception of Virginia, the states gradually repealed laws that interfered with the collection of British debts. In Massachusetts, the legislature suspended interest accrued during the war on prewar loans in 1784, but the law recognized that "real British subjects" and "absentees" (i.e., Loyalists) in Article VI were entitled to the principal. It also made clear that, should Congress determine that the obligation to pay included wartime interest, the states' courts would honor its decision.[42] In western Massachusetts, the state's attentiveness to creditor rights, domestic as well as foreign, contributed to the regional tax revolt known as Shays's Rebellion.

Because merchants in Boston and the eastern ports were creditors themselves, they were eager to reestablish trade with Britain. They supported forcing debtors to pay what they owed.[43] Among the beneficiaries was Mary Hayley (sister of English Patriot John Wilkes and widow of London oil merchant George Hayley), who spent eight years in Boston collecting nearly £100,000 that merchants and shopkeepers in New England and Pennsylvania owed her late husband. According to a list compiled by a group of London merchants, the estate's outstanding balance had fallen to £79,599 by 1791. Hayley's absence from subsequent creditor lists suggests that she succeeded in settling the rest.[44]

Yet even in states where creditor rights appeared secure, courts were slow to enforce the peace, and the justice they dispensed was often incomplete. During Shays's Rebellion, insurgents in Exeter, New Hampshire, surrounded the statehouse where the assembly was sitting and demanded that it repudiate the obligation in Article IV to repay British debts.[45] Speaking of the prevalence of such attitudes, the author of a Scottish summary of American law warned that plaintiffs "may be considered fortunate in obtaining judgment at the end of three years." And that was only if they had "the good luck to get over the frowns of the Bench, and the unpopularity which is sure to be stamped upon [their] character." The tract closed with a letter from President of the Confederation Congress Arthur St. Clair, written during the spring of 1787, calling on the states to repeal all remaining laws in conflict with the treaty. The request was partly a question of national honor. Should the Union continue to default on its treaty obligations, however, the standoff could become the difference between war and peace. "Contracting nations cannot, like individuals, avail themselves of Courts of Justice," St. Clair warned, "yet an appeal to Heaven and to arms, is always in their power, and often in their inclination." Unless they were prepared for renewed hostilities, state governments had no choice but to enforce the peace.[46]

A Treaty-Worthy Government

By the time St. Clair penned his letter, most states had selected delegates for the federal convention that gathered in Philadelphia on May 25, 1787. In the revealing words of David Hendrickson, the Constitution that resulted was a "peace pact" designed to preserve harmonious relations between the Union's 13 members. But the new coalition was also a "solid coercive union," as Hamilton had described his ideal federation in 1780, which Federalists hoped would do a better job of maintaining peace with other governments.[47] Under the Articles of Confederation, Congress envisioned the United States as a continental "league of friendship"[48]— one that Americans expected someday to include Canada and the rest of British North America.

Neither Canada nor any of Britain's other colonies appeared in the new Constitution, however, nor did the words "friend" or "friendship." Although Congress could still admit new states, the "more perfect Union" in the charter's preamble was no longer an alliance between sovereign states, each with its own people and populist interests.[49] It became a unitary empire bounded by the Treaty of Paris's limits—a union with "one people," in the words of the Declaration's first paragraph, and with many of the coercive powers that had once belonged to the British king and Parliament. True to Hamilton's vision, Americans were now subject to congressional taxation, they had to accept treaties and treaty-sanctioned borders as the "Law of the Land," and they could be compelled in federal courts to honor their foreign obligations.[50]

The result was a "treaty-worthy" government finally capable of fulfilling its international obligations, including, as promised in the Declaration, to Britain.[51] To be sure, neither Hamilton nor anyone else predicted that the "candid world" to which Congress addressed the Declaration was about to change, practically beyond recognition, amid the cataclysm of the French Revolution. In the controversial Anglo-American Treaty of Amity, Commerce, and Navigation, which Jay negotiated in London during the fall of 1794, the United States achieved many, though by no means all, of the Treaty of Paris's unrealized objectives. The most important were a timeline for handing over the western posts, a joint commission to settle the remaining American debts to British creditors, and another commission to clarify the Canadian border.[52] But because Britain was at war with France, peace with the Union's oldest enemy proved impossible without upsetting relations with its oldest ally.

Between 1798 and 1800, the Adams administration found itself in an undeclared naval war with the French Republic, the so-called Franco-American Quasi-War. That was followed during the Jefferson and Madison administrations by renewed conflict with Britain. In 1812, differences between the two culminated in a second Anglo-American war. Lasting peace would remain a distant hope for America until it returned to Europe in 1815.[53]

One consequence of the wars triggered by the French Revolution was a powerful animus against what Washington in his Farewell Address (1796) called "permanent alliances," especially in Europe.[54] That did not mean, however, that Americans were able (or willing) to escape foreign entanglements in the form of maritime trade; transatlantic investment in their canals, railroads, and factories; and immigration. In 1807, acting in concert with Britain, Congress made forced migration from Africa illegal. But migrants from Ireland, southern and eastern Europe, and Asia would flock in growing numbers to the United States' shores, turning the republic of the farmers into an industrial superpower. The United States was also unable to avoid the obligations that peace and friendship with other governments, especially Britain, placed on its banks, corporations, and courts.[55] During the century between Waterloo and Sarajevo, Americans had no need for formal engagements comparable to the Franco-American alliance of 1778 or the British entente that followed the Jay Treaty, but that was largely because Europe was at peace.

The collapse of that global order in 1914 and again in 1940 drew the United States inexorably back into Europe's military and diplomatic vortex. Historians sometimes describe NATO's creation in 1949 as a second "American revolution." Although the phrase captures the significance of abandoning the "tradition of non-entanglement" that Washington championed in his Farewell Address, the peace and security that NATO has ensured since its creation is just as clearly a fulfillment of the Declaration's promise to draw a sharp line between how Americans treat their enemies in war and their friends in peace.[56]

So, too, however, is the populist unilateralism that has been an equally powerful impulse in American international relations. During the French Revolutionary Wars, Americans' continental ambitions of 1776, which Hamilton and the Federalists thought the Constitution had laid to rest, reappeared on a grander and far more disruptive scale than even Franklin, the most expansionist of the founders, could have imagined.[57] In an 1803 agreement, the legality of which is still questioned by constitutional historians, Jefferson doubled the Union's size by purchasing the former Spanish territory of Louisiana from Napoleon Bonaparte.[58] A decade later, the War of 1812 produced several more attempts by the Madison administration on Canada. James Monroe, the third member of the Virginia dynasty, annexed Spanish Florida between 1819 and 1821 and extended the border with Spain's dominion of Mexico to the Pacific.

In Florida, the key actor was Andrew Jackson, whose unauthorized invasion acted as an accelerant on the founders' unilateralist and expansionist fantasies, helping forge a "Jacksonian tradition" that has been part of American war and diplomacy ever since.[59] The Tennessee caudillo's chief enabler during the Florida crisis was Secretary of State John Quincy Adams. The last two presidents to serve in the Revolutionary War—Adams as a diplomat in Europe and Jackson in a unit of South Carolina partisans—shared the founding generation's commitment to making peace by dominating and, where possible, absorbing the Union's neighbors.[60]

Peace, of course, was not the outcome of acquiring either Louisiana or Florida. Although the Florida purchase closed a loophole in the illegal slave trade, the First Seminole War set the stage for a second and equally brutal war in the 1830s against the native people who composed most of the former Spanish colony's population. Meanwhile, in what Jefferson famously likened to the ringing of "a fire bell in the night," Louisiana threatened the founders' sordid compromise over how far slavery, which the Northwest Ordinance had banned above the Ohio River, should be allowed to expand.[61] Resolved in 1820 by the Missouri Compromise, the question returned more virulently (and violently), as Jefferson feared, with the admission of Texas in 1845 and the conquest of Upper California and the rest of Mexico's northern half.

Instead of bringing peace, James Polk's "wicked war," as Amy Greenberg has called it,[62] led inexorably to the Civil War—and, eventually, to the Union's "second founding" and Reconstruction. The century closed with an invitation from Rudyard Kipling, poet laureate of the British Empire, for the former British colonies to "take up the White Man's burden" in the Pacific.[63] The McKinley administration accepted, producing an overseas empire that, by the time of William McKinley's death, included Alaska, Hawaii, and a second batch of Spanish colonies, stretching from Puerto Rico to the Philippines. Without that empire, it is not possible to imagine the global war that Americans waged between 1941 and 1945, nor the regional conflicts that followed in Korea, Vietnam, Afghanistan, and Iraq.

Navigating War and Peace

If the postwar alliance system and the United States' continental and transpacific expansion were (and are) both consistent, albeit in different ways, with the language in the Declaration, the document's most enduring international legacy is surely its ringing endorsement of government based on "the consent of the governed." No one grasped the imperative to align the Union's foreign relations with its citizens' needs and wishes more clearly than Washington did. In a revealing 1790 letter to English historian Catharine Macaulay, written near the end of his first year in office, the president reflected on what he termed "the last great experiment, for promoting human happiness, by reasonable compact." For the experiment to succeed, the new polity was necessarily "a government of accomodation as well as a government of Laws." Realist that he was, Washington did not deny there would be times that required force at home and abroad, but he saw an equally compelling need for accommodation and compromise. "Much was to be done by *prudence*, much by *conciliation*, much by *firmness*," he told his friend. (Emphasis in original.) In a union founded on the sovereignty of the people, the only way to get anything done was to govern using all three approaches.[64]

Washington's dedication to finding common ground with all Americans, whether they agreed with him or not, is worth remembering. But so, too, is Bentham's warning about the Declaration's hostility to all governments, including the one the founders created. When he wrote Macaulay, Washington had recently returned from a monthlong tour of New England. Venturing as far as Portsmouth, New Hampshire, he was pleased to see outbound ships laden with grain from a "remarkably good" harvest and the growth of manufacturing. People everywhere seemed "uncommonly well pleased with their situation and prospects." Washington knew, however, that the Union's fortunes could easily change, with the developing revolution in France being a particular worry. Although the Marquis de Lafayette's involvement was cause for hope, Washington's "greatest fear" was that France's reformers would not be "sufficiently cool and moderate."[65] By inflaming opinions on both sides of the aisle, crises in Europe and elsewhere, the president scarcely needed to say, could upset the delicate balance upon which the Union's domestic peace depended.

As Washington articulated most fully in his Farewell Address, the connection between foreign policy and domestic politics would complicate the rest of that president's time in office and bedevil his successors. The 1798 Alien Enemies Act, adopted amid Federalists' overwrought fears of foreign subversion during the Quasi-War with France, has recently reappeared as a threat to the rule of law and the Constitution. When it was enacted, the Adams administration's Democratic-Republican opponents denounced the law in nearly identical terms to those employed by its critics in our time. There are questions as to whether even Adams supported it. Given his druthers, wrote Stanley Elkins and Eric McKitrick, the second president's "sense of his own position as Chief Magistrate disposed him to prefer consent to coercion," which the first president had preferred too.[66]

And that, in the end, is a warning against placing too much stock in what the Declaration of Independence has to say about war, peace, and America's relations with other nations. Although the founders showed themselves willing and able to make the compromises that peace with Britain required, the clearest evidence for that willingness is in the Treaty of Paris and the Constitution, not the Declaration. Of the Declaration's 1,000-plus words, the vast majority are about the justness of the war that George III and his British subjects forced Americans to embrace. Simply put, the Declaration is a call to arms. Given the gravity of the Union's military situation in 1776, that was as it should have been. But the Declaration was (and is) less useful as a roadmap for peace and friendship. Not only does it say nothing about the concessions that ending the Revolutionary War with anything other than unconditional victory was bound to entail, but the 27 charges against the British king and his subjects were hard to square with the peace that Congress proclaimed as its goal.

As the Union's early history shows, the founding generation found the tension between war and peace—between knowing when to stand up and fight and when to sit down and negotiate—difficult, though not impossible, to resolve. In our current neo-Jacksonian moment and in years to come, surely the only way to manage that tension is by showing the same wisdom and foresight.

Notes

1. Richard Henry Lee, "Resolution of Independence Moved by R. H. Lee for the Virginia Delegation," Founders Online, June 7, 1776, https://founders.archives.gov/documents/Jefferson/01-01-02-0159; and Thomas Paine, "Common Sense," in *The Complete Writings of Thomas Paine*, ed. Philip S. Foner (Citadel Press, 1945), 1:43, https://cdn.mises.org/The%20Complete%20Writings%20of%20Thomas%20Paine%2C%20Volume%201_2.pdf.

2. Continental Congress, "IV. The Declaration as Adopted by Congress," July 6, 1775, https://founders.archives.gov/documents/Jefferson/01-01-02-0113-0005.

3. Worthington Chauncey Ford, ed., *Journals of the Continental Congress, 1774–1789*, vol. 2, *1775: May 10–September 20* (Government Printing Office, 1905), 144–45, 147, 150–51, 153, 155.

4. George Washington, "Letter to the Inhabitants of Canada," Founders Online, September 14, 1775, https://founders.archives.gov/documents/Washington/03-01-02-0358.

5. Worthington Chauncey Ford, ed., *Journals of the Continental Congress, 1774–1789*, vol. 1, *1774* (Government Printing Office, 1904), 111; Ford, ed., *Journals of the Continental Congress*, 2:68–70; and Worthington Chauncey Ford, ed., *Journals of the Continental Congress 1774–1789*, vol. 3, *1775: September 21–December 30* (Government Printing Office, 1905), 85–86.

6. Jeffers Lennox, *North of America: Loyalists, Indigenous Nations, and the Borders of the Long American Revolution* (Yale University Press, 2022), 19–59.

7. "The First National Constitution: The Articles of Confederation (Mar. 1, 1781)," in *Colonies to Nation, 1763–1789: A Documentary History of the American Revolution*, ed. Jack P. Greene (W. W. Norton, 1975), 434; and Eliga H. Gould, *Among the Powers of the Earth: The American Revolution and the Making of a New World Empire* (Harvard University Press, 2012), 2.

8. Ford, ed., *Journals of the Continental Congress, 1774–1789*, 2:182.

9. Benjamin Franklin, "Proposed Articles of Confederation," Founders Online, ca. July 21, 1775, https://founders.archives.gov/documents/Franklin/01-22-02-0069; and Yale Law School, Lillian Goldman Law Library, Avalon Project, "Treaty with the Delawares: 1778," https://avalon.law.yale.edu/18th_century/del1778.asp.

10. Alan Taylor, *The Divided Ground: Indians, Settlers, and the Northern Borderland of the American Revolution* (Alfred A. Knopf, 2006), 111–22.

11. Paul H. Smith, "The American Loyalists: Notes on Their Organization and Numerical Strength," *The William and Mary Quarterly* 25, no. 2 (1968): 269, https://www.jstor.org/stable/1919095.

12. Thomas Paine, "The American Crisis I," in Foner, *The Complete Writings of Thomas Paine*, 1:49, 53.

13. Lisa Ford, *The King's Peace: Law and Order in the British Empire* (Harvard University Press, 2021), 24–57; and *The New Encyclopedia of Southern Culture*, vol. 24, *Race* (2013), under "Lynching and Racial Violence."

14. Maya Jasanoff, *Liberty's Exiles: American Loyalists in the Revolutionary World* (Vintage Books, 2012), 21–53.

15. "To Suppress 'Rebellion and Sedition': Royal Proclamation of Rebellion (Aug. 26, 1775)," in Greene, *Colonies to Nation, 1763–1789*, 259.

16. John Lind, *An Answer to the Declaration of the American Congress*, 4th ed. (London, 1776), 131–32; and David Armitage, "The Declaration of Independence and International Law," *The William and Mary Quarterly* 59, no. 1 (2002): 52–54, https://www.jstor.org/stable/3491637.

17. Ralph Waldo Emerson, "Concord Hymn," July 4, 1837, Poetry Foundation, https://www.poetryfoundation.org/poems/45870/concord-hymn.

18. John Shy, *A People Numerous and Armed: Reflections on the Military Struggle for American Independence*, rev. ed. (University of Michigan Press, 1990), 163–79.

19. Richard B. Morris, *The Peacemakers: The Great Powers and American Independence* (Harper & Row, 1965), 275–86, 412.

20. Winslow C. Watson, ed., *Men and Times of the Revolution* [. . .], 2nd ed. (New York), 204, 206.

21. "Peace: The Treaty of Paris (Sept. 3, 1783)," in Greene, *Colonies to Nation, 1763–1789*, 418–22; and Gordon S. Wood, *Empire of Liberty: A History of the Early Republic, 1789–1815* (Oxford University Press, 2009).

22. "Peace," in Greene, *Colonies to Nation, 1763–1789*, 421; James H. Kettner, "Subjects or Citizens? A Note on British Views Respecting the Legal Effects of American Independence," *Virginia Law Review* 62, no. 5 (1976): 945–67, https://www.jstor.org/stable/1072398; and Katherine A. Kellock, "London Merchants and the Pre-1776 American Debts," *Guildhall Studies in London History* 1, no. 3 (1974): 109.

23. Eliga H. Gould, "Sheffield's Vision: The American Revolution and the 1783 Partition of North America," in *Making the British Empire, 1660–1800*, ed. Jason Peacey (Manchester University Press, 2020), 161, 174–76.

24. Eliga H. Gould, "As Far as the Canaries? Longitude, Prize Law, and the Anglo-American Armistice of 1783," presentation, After 1776: Opportunities, Shocks, and Dangers, Thomas Jefferson's Monticello, Robert H. Smith International Center for Jefferson Studies, Charlottesville, VA, October 2024.

25. "Peace," in Greene, *Colonies to Nation, 1763–1789*, 422.

26. Maurice Morgann, "Note on Article 7 of Definitive Treaty," 1786, vol. 87b, fol. 391v, William Petty, 1st Marquis of Lansdowne, 2nd Earl of Shelburne Papers, William L. Clements Library, University of Michigan; and Cassandra Pybus, *Epic Journeys of Freedom: Runaway Slaves of the American Revolution and Their Global Quest for Liberty* (Beacon Press, 2007), 1–6, 61–69.

27. "Peace," in Greene, *Colonies to Nation, 1763–1789*, 422.

28. Michael A. Blaakman, *Speculation Nation: Land Mania in the Revolutionary American Republic* (University of Pennsylvania Press, 2023).

29. Charles R. Ritcheson, *Aftermath of Revolution: British Policy Toward the United States, 1783–1795* (Southern Methodist University Press, 1969), 75–81.

30. Charles F. Hobson, "The Recovery of British Debts in the Federal Circuit Court of Virginia, 1790 to 1797," *Virginia Magazine of History and Biography* 92, no. 2 (1984): 179, https://www.jstor.org/stable/4248711; and Herbert E. Sloan, *Principle and Interest: Thomas Jefferson and the Problem of Debt* (Oxford University Press, 1995).

31. John Adams et al., "Preliminary Peace Treaty Between the United States and Great Britain," Founders Online, November 30, 1782, https://founders.archives.gov/documents/Adams/06-14-02-0058.

32. Peter H. Lindert and Jeffrey G. Williamson, *Unequal Gains: American Growth and Inequality Since 1700* (Princeton University Press, 2016), 85.

33. Curtis P. Nettels, *The Economic History of the United States*, vol. 2, *The Emergence of a National Economy, 1775–1815* (Holt, Rinehart and Winston, 1962), 60–61, 87; and Thomas M. Doerflinger, *A Vigorous Spirit of Enterprise: Merchants and Economic Development in Revolutionary Philadelphia* (University of North Carolina Press, 1986), 263.

34. National Archives Foundation, "Treaty of Fort Stanwix," https://docsteach.org/document/treaty-fort-stanwix/.

35. Ned Blackhawk, *The Rediscovery of America: Native Peoples and the Unmaking of U.S. History* (Yale University Press, 2023), 176–204.

36. "Toward the Creation of New States: The Northwest Ordinance (July 13, 1787)," in Greene, *Colonies to Nation, 1763–1789*, 473; and Eric Hinderaker, *Elusive Empires: Constructing Colonialism in the Ohio Valley, 1673–1800* (Cambridge University Press, 1997), 228, 231, 236, 242, 247, 255–56.

37. Merrill Jensen, *The New Nation: A History of the United States During the Confederation, 1781–1789* (Vintage Books, 1950), 282–301.

38. Frederick W. Marks III, *Independence on Trial: Foreign Affairs and the Making of the Constitution* (Louisiana State University Press, 1973), 52–95.

39. Thomas Paine, "A Supernumerary Crisis," in Foner, *The Complete Writings of Thomas Paine*, 1:237–38.

40. Melancton Smith et al., *An Address from the Committee Appointed at Mrs. Vandewater's on the 13th Day of September, 1784* [. . .] (New York, 1784), https://name.umdl.umich.edu/N14462.0001.001.

41. David A. Weinstein, "*Rutgers v. Waddington*: Alexander Hamilton and the Birth Pangs of Judicial Review," *Judicial Notice* 9 (Summer 2013): 27–34, https://history.nycourts.gov/wp-content/uploads/2019/01/Judicial-Notice-09.pdf.

42. *A Collection of Acts or Laws Passed in the State of Massachusetts Bay* [. . .] (London, 1785), 34–35.

43. Leonard L. Richards, *Shays's Rebellion: The American Revolution's Final Battle* (University of Pennsylvania Press, 2002).

44. "State of Claims of British Merchants Trading to America," British National Archives, February 5, 1791; and Amanda Bowie Moniz, "A Radical Shrew in America," *Commonplace*, April 2008, https://commonplace.online/article/a-radical-shrew-in-america/.

45. W. Jeffrey Bolster, "'The Absurdity of Nonresistance': Reexamining Article 10 of New Hampshire's Constitution, the 'Right of Revolution,'" *Historical New Hampshire*, Fall

2007, https://nhhistory.org/object/58069/the-absurdity-of-nonresistance-reexamining-article-10-of-new-hampshire-s-constitution-the-righ.

46. A *Summary Review of the Laws of the United States of North-America* [. . .] (Edinburgh, Scotland, 1788), 6, 45.

47. David C. Hendrickson, *Peace Pact: The Lost World of the American Founding* (University Press of Kansas, 2003); and Alexander Hamilton to James Duane, September 3, 1780, Founders Online, https://founders.archives.gov/documents/Hamilton/01-02-02-0838.

48. "The First National Constitution," in Greene, *Colonies to Nation, 1763–1789*, 429.

49. US Const. pmbl.

50. US Const. art. VI.

51. Gould, *Among the Powers of the Earth*, 139–44.

52. Stanley M. Elkins and Eric McKitrick, *The Age of Federalism: The Early American Republic, 1788–1800* (Oxford University Press, 1993), 406–14.

53. Bradford Perkins, *The Cambridge History of American Foreign Relations*, vol. 1, *The Creation of a Republican Empire, 1776–1865* (Cambridge University Press, 1993), 105–7, 111–46.

54. Felix Gilbert, *To the Farewell Address: Ideas of Early American Foreign Policy* (Princeton University Press, 1961).

55. Daniel Hulsebosch, "Independence and Union: Imperfect Unions in Revolutionary Anglo-America," in Mark Philip Bradley, ed., *The Cambridge History of America and the World*, vol. 1, *1500–1820*, ed. Eliga H. Gould et al. (Cambridge University Press, 2022), 504–7.

56. Lawrence S. Kaplan, *The United States and NATO: The Formative Years* (University Press of Kentucky, 1984), 1.

57. Gerald Stourzh, *Benjamin Franklin and American Foreign Policy* (University of Chicago Press, 1954), 142–46, 183–84.

58. Mark Peterson, *The Making and Breaking of the American Constitution: A Thousand-Year History* (Princeton University Press, forthcoming), pts. III and IV.

59. Walter Russell Mead, "The Jacksonian Tradition and American Foreign Policy," *The National Interest*, Winter 1999–2000, 5–29, https://www.jstor.org/stable/42897216.

60. James E. Lewis, *The American Union and the Problem of Neighborhood: The United States and the Collapse of the Spanish Empire, 1783–1829* (University of North Carolina Press, 1998); and Deborah A. Rosen, *Border Law: The First Seminole War and American Nationhood* (Harvard University Press, 2015).

61. Thomas Jefferson to John Holmes, April 22, 1820, Founders Online, https://founders.archives.gov/documents/Jefferson/03-15-02-0518.

62. Amy S. Greenberg, *A Wicked War: Polk, Clay, Lincoln, and the 1846 U.S. Invasion of Mexico* (Vintage Books, 2012); and Eric Foner, *The Second Founding: How the Civil War and Reconstruction Remade the Constitution* (W. W. Norton, 2019).

63. Rudyard Kipling, "The White Man's Burden," February 4, 1899, Kipling Society, https://www.kiplingsociety.co.uk/poem/poems_burden.htm.

64. George Washington to Catharine Sawbridge Macaulay Graham, January 9, 1790, Founders Online, https://founders.archives.gov/documents/Washington/05-04-02-0363; and Yuval Levin, *American Covenant: How the Constitution Unified Our Nation—and Could Again* (Basic Books, 2024).

65. Washington to Graham.

66. Elkins and McKitrick, *The Age of Federalism*, 590.

6

Founding American Foreign Policy

WALTER RUSSELL MEAD

The establishment of a distinctly American approach to foreign policy, an approach that remains central to American debates even today, is one of the greatest and one of the least appreciated achievements of the American founding.

The founders' views on foreign policy were more central to their achievements than we generally acknowledge. Foreign policy is not an extraneous topic that the founders engaged once they'd settled the more pressing business of domestic affairs. Their ideas about international relations helped them define the kind of state that the Constitution needed to build. And without their concerns about the intentions of potentially hostile foreign powers, the Constitution, had one been adopted at all, would almost certainly have established a much weaker central government.

Contributing to the lack of appreciation of the founders' achievement in foreign policy is the confusion caused by the shifts in American foreign policy thinking during the 20th century. As the American superpower took on a progressively larger global role, opponents of that trend invoked George Washington's Farewell Address to support a policy of isolationism. So prestigious was that remarkable address that the isolationists' opposition preferred to argue that, while Washington's words were wise in his day, so much had changed since the time of the founders that their foreign policy ideas were no longer applicable. The result was to establish two false beliefs in the minds of three generations of foreign policy thinkers. The first was that the founders cared little for foreign affairs. The second was that there were few or no meaningful precedents or patterns in the pre–World War II era, including the time of the founding, on which contemporary makers of foreign policy needed to reflect.

The impoverished sense of history these errors produced has contributed significantly to the poor performance of the American foreign policy class in the years since the fall of the Soviet Union. And the failure to ground contemporary American foreign policy in a respected and legitimate national tradition is costly. Grounding the foreign policy of today in the wisdom of the past and placing contemporary debates in a richer historical and intellectual context will make for better policies, better debates, and stronger public understanding of the choices that political leaders ultimately make.

Ignoring the Founders

There are several reasons why it was relatively easy for post–World War II globalists to consign the foreign policy traditions stretching back to the founders to the dustbin of history.

First, the founders' approach emerged from more than a quarter century of contentious debate rather than from a single, compressed process that would focus the attention of historians. There was no Philadelphia convention on national strategy. Some of the Federalist Papers addressed the roles that the various branches were designed to play, but none of the founders wrote a series of authoritative state papers to provide a definitive description of the intellectual framework behind the new nation's engagement in the world. Washington's Farewell Address is as close as any founder ever came to making a direct and succinct statement of the principles that guided their approach, but even that speech was directed more toward attacking Thomas Jefferson's views of US-French relations than at offering a candid and comprehensive exposition of the intellectual foundations of American statecraft.

Second, while several important essays in the Federalist Papers address foreign policy issues, the connection between the structure of the American government and the nature of American foreign policy remained largely obscure. America's emerging international strategy was less the product of a single process of conscious reasoning than a set of precedents and examples developed over time by statesmen whose sharp and sometimes even bitter political differences were contained within some widely shared cultural and political assumptions. The actual policies of the founding era were, like most actions of most statesmen, driven more by what Harold Macmillan is said to have referred to as "events, dear boy, events" than by the intellectual necessities of a consciously held grand idea.[1] The founders did not go back to a manual of statecraft to make their foreign policy. They reflected on the events of the day through the lens of a set of ideas about history, human nature, the American republic, and the nature of international society of which they were not always fully aware.

Finally, like the Constitution itself, the emergent foreign policy of the early republic was less the product of a single controlling intelligence than the result of compromise among a variety of viewpoints. American foreign policy was elicited by responses to the pressures of the passing day, expressed in action, not theoretical explanation, and it rested on a succession of perpetually adjusted working compromises between often-antagonistic approaches rather than the consistent implementation of a single set of ideas.

The early American leaders disagreed, often bitterly, over foreign policy, and indeed, disagreements between Jefferson and Alexander Hamilton over foreign policy contributed to the creation of the first political parties in the republic's history. New England's Federalists were driven to the brink of secession by their opposition to Jefferson's embargo in 1807 and James Madison's War of 1812. Andrew Jackson's obstreperous expansionism appalled the more decorous members of the young republic's diplomatic establishment.

Nevertheless, a pattern of underlying strategic consensus gradually emerged. By the time then–Secretary of State John Quincy Adams drafted President James Monroe's response to Britain's proposal for an

Anglo-American joint guarantee of the new Latin American states' independence, the Americans had found an approach to international affairs that for the most part still guides us 200 years later.

This is not a unitary tradition. No simple body of doctrine could suffice for the needs of a dramatically growing and changing republic like the United States during a revolutionary and transformative era in world affairs like the past 250 years. The Constitution is not a set of municipal ordinances to be mechanistically enforced. It is a system for generating laws whose integrity we seek to maintain. The American foreign policy tradition similarly is less a rigid set of policies to be mechanically followed under all circumstances than a way of generating new policies in response to the flow of events.

The ability to accommodate contention and competition within a stable institutional framework was the hallmark of American statesmanship during the American founding, and just as the Constitution incorporated often contrasting ideas and aspirations into the foundations of American governance, an American approach to foreign policy emerged from the debates and contests of the first decades of American independence.

The founders saw foreign and domestic affairs as closely connected, and in their view, the tasks of organizing a suitable governing apparatus and philosophy for their new nation could not be separated from the question of how that new nation was to interact with the world. It would be foolish to construct a government capable of managing its internal affairs that was too weak or too disunited to define and defend the nation's interests abroad, and as even many critics of the strong federal system adopted in Philadelphia came to appreciate, the need to present a strong, united front to the world would require a more effective and centralized national government than Americans might otherwise have chosen to establish.

For Americans today, examining the founders' integrated approach is more than an exercise in historical scholarship. Our increasingly turbulent times are forcing us to return to first principles in both domestic and foreign affairs; we will benefit by seeing how our predecessors approached similar problems in their own revolutionary era.

In what follows, I will try to outline key elements in the unwritten constitution that guides the development of American national strategy by looking at how the founders coped with the issues that immediately began to confront the former colonies as their independence was recognized. In times like the present, when Americans are asking basic questions about the nature and purpose of our foreign policy, a deeper appreciation of our heritage may help sharpen, clarify, and even to some degree resolve our contemporary debates.

Competitive Statecraft

In framing the Constitution, the founders were engaging, inevitably, in competitive statecraft. They were not only designing a state that could withstand the centrifugal pressures arising from the frequently diverging priorities and values of the new union's 13 members. They were building a state that could defend its territorial integrity and independence and advance its interests in the extremely competitive world of late 18th-century world politics.

The American Revolution was, after all, an episode in what is often called the Second Hundred Years' War, a series of increasingly violent and expensive conflicts between Great Britain and France as the two European superpowers competed to control the key power centers in an emergent global arena. From the War of the League of Augsburg, beginning in 1689, through the Napoleonic Wars, ending at Waterloo in 1815, Britain, France, and their respective European and global allies fought a series of bloody wars across the world. Anglo-French competition would touch every continent except Antarctica, and the consequences of Britain's ultimate victory are still reverberating around the world today.

This long-running conflict was a principal driver of American history, and it shaped the political outlook and individual careers of many members of the founding generation. Washington's older brother named the family seat Mount Vernon after his commander, a British admiral. Worries over the impact of the Seven Years' War on Britain's national debt led Parliament to tax the colonies, while the colonists' sense of security following the conquest of French Canada helped give them the courage to resist and fed their hopes that they could govern themselves without the protection of the British Crown. Washington, whose actions as a young officer in 1753 helped ignite the Seven Years' War and whose victory at Yorktown was made possible by the timely arrival of a French fleet, saw his presidential administration almost destroyed as Napoleonic France mounted its climactic challenge to British power.

America was born in war, and the framers of its institutions sought to make their new state strong enough to survive the shocks and assaults of a series of global conflicts that inevitably would threaten the commerce and the security of the young transatlantic republic.

Historians and policymakers endlessly debate the meaning and the salience of terms like "strategy," "grand strategy," and "national strategy," and in reality there is not much hope for consensus on what these terms mean, what differentiates the different levels of strategy, or indeed whether terms like grand strategy correspond to anything real. Nevertheless, we can see in both antiquity and the modern world important linkages among the ways states are built, the societies that build them, and the resources and methods different states bring to their international engagements.

In the ancient world, Sparta's reliance on helots to support a well-trained and well-disciplined warrior elite shaped its goals and policies during much of its existence. The Spartan army was a formidable force, making Sparta close to invincible in ordinary land battles. But invincibility had its limits. The number of Spartiates, as the elite were called, was small, and the fallen could not be quickly replaced. Fear of helot insurrection meant that a significant proportion of the city's forces needed to be kept close to home. And the lack of a commercial class limited Sparta's economic potential.

Carthage brought a different mix of strengths and weaknesses to the table. Its mercantile character gave it sea power, a wide geographic base, and the abilities to recover from setbacks and generate large resources when needed. Its political system was flexible enough to allow considerable personal initiative. Hamilcar Barca and his sons Hannibal and Hasdrubal were able to build a flourishing province in Spain that revived Carthaginian power following the First Punic War. But the system of decentralized leadership that gave the Barcids autonomy also worked against Carthage during the Second Punic War. Hannibal fought almost as a freelancer, and political rivals in Carthage forestalled any efforts to provide his forces in Italy with the support that would have allowed him to turn battlefield victories into the conquest of Rome.

The Roman Republic, by contrast, developed an extraordinary base of strong institutions that allowed it to survive the foreign assaults, of which Hannibal's was the most serious, and contain the ambitions of domestic politicians long enough for the republic to conquer the Mediterranean world before succumbing to forces that transformed it into an empire. Beset by enemies outside the walls in the thickly settled, agriculturally fertile region of central Italy and riven internally by strife between rich and poor and among aristocratic clans struggling for supremacy, Rome by necessity developed political institutions that could tame domestic rivalries and maintain the strong military organization required by a state of perpetual danger. Not even Hannibal's sweeping victories over a series of Roman armies could shake the foundations of Roman power.

In these cases, and many more, states acquired their characteristic strengths and weaknesses from the cultural, geographic, and geopolitical milieus of their formative years. The remembered history (sometimes embedded in mythology) and cultural preferences of a given population combined with the physical and political geography of its society and neighborhood to produce a political and strategic character that both enabled and limited its ability to manage its domestic and international affairs. In many cases, this process was "natural," which is to say the result of time and chance, producing a set of customs and practices sometimes attributed to a mythical founder or reformer. But there are cases, like that of Solon's reforms in Athens, in which the impact of an individual is historically attested. In Roman history, the mythical King Numa is said to have given Rome its original laws. Centuries later, we can see how Augustus transformed the dying republic into a principate.

Managing the complex interplay among the culture (with religion very much included) of a given people, the economic and technological base that supports that people's existence and to some degree determines its outlook and forms its institutions, and the international environment in which it finds itself constitutes the demanding art of government. No one accomplishes this task to perfection; this is one reason Enoch Powell's observation that "all political lives . . . end in failure" holds up so well.[2]

Many, perhaps most, political leaders are simply policymakers, attempting to meet the exigencies of the hour without devoting much thought to the architecture of ideas and institutions in which they move. Some, whose statues in the temple of fame are often more imposing, bring a richer awareness to their political work. Whether one thinks of Pericles developing a war strategy for Athens, Elizabeth I placing Protestant England on a stable foundation, or Abraham Lincoln leading the United States through our Civil War, these statesmen and stateswomen leave deep footprints in the sands of time.

Many of the American founders proved to be excellent statesmen, but they belonged to an even more august body. They did not just manage the affairs of a state. They founded one. That state endured, and not just because the Constitution served Americans well in their domestic affairs. It endured as well because the founders' republic gave the American state a distinctive and distinctively successful method of conducting its foreign affairs.

In this the founders succeeded beyond their expectations. Many believed that foreign policy would be the weakest point in the American government. But as it happened, the country that declared independence in 1776 and inaugurated a constitutional order 13 years later has for 250 years defended its integrity and advanced its interests with greater success than any government in the modern era.

To understand that accomplishment, we'll look first at the way the American Constitution created a state with its own approach for identifying and acting on the national interest and then at the emergence of a distinctively American tradition of foreign policy during the long period when the framers of the Constitution remained at the helm of American government.

The Mirror State

Few phrases are used as widely or cavalierly as "national interest," yet it is not very easy to say what the national interest actually is, and the question of how a given state discerns its national interest is one of the most consequential issues in statecraft. Historically, a number of states in Europe and elsewhere identified their national interest with the perceived interest of a ruling dynasty or a faction within it. The oligarchic, mercantile Italian states like Venice and Genoa generally saw their interests through the medium of trade—and, often, the specific trading interests of the dominant political faction of the day.

In today's world, we see a wide variety in the way states perceive their national interest and the method by which the choice is made between alternative views of that interest. China, Iran, North Korea, and Russia think about national interest in quite different ways. Economic interest is a more dominant factor in Chinese thinking than in the thinking of the other revisionist powers. For governments like North Korea, Russia, and, for that matter, Cuba, regime survival demonstrably matters far more than conventional ideas about economic interest. Vladimir Putin holds a theory of statecraft and geopolitical competition with deep roots in Russian history. Many of his opponents in the European Union operate on an entirely different conception of the national interest, built precisely on a repudiation of the historical notions of state power and competition that currently shape the Kremlin's perceptions.

It is not, as in the journalistic cliché, that some strategists are playing checkers while others are playing chess or even multidimensional chess. It is that some states are playing Parcheesi, others paddleball, and still others Monopoly. Some actors chase the dreams of past glory; some seek to remake the world in the image of a favored ideology. Some want to exalt their national identity and perhaps recover lost territory or avenge past slights. Some want to transcend the dreary rounds of struggle and war that have marred human history so grievously in order to build a new international order that will end war forever. Some believe that "transnational" issues like climate change override national interests as historically understood.

And these differences of opinion about the definition of the national interest don't exist just among states. The definition of the national interest is controversial within every state. Even totalitarian states like Mao Zedong's China and Josef Stalin's Soviet Union saw continual debate over what the regime should do in response to the various opportunities and threats that different groups in the regime perceive—or think they do. How much weight should be given to the need to remain faithful to the ideological commitments of the ruling ideology? How much is to be gained, and how much to be feared, from engagement with opponents and rivals?

American foreign policy is as subject to these ideological and pragmatic debates as that of any other country, and given the regional, economic, and cultural diversity of the country, these debates can be even sharper and more divisive here than in many places. If New England were an independent country, its foreign policy would differ substantially from that of a Republic of Texas. Iowa would not see eye to eye with Oregon, and Florida and Michigan would bring very different priorities to their foreign policies if they were independent states. These differences were already apparent at the time of the Declaration of Independence and have become only more marked during the succeeding years.

To understand the American founding's contributions to American foreign policy, one must therefore look at the way the structure of the American governing system devised in the Constitution gave the United States a method of adjudicating the inevitable debates over the nature of the national interest and the steps most likely to advance that interest in a competitive world.

The most common method of conducting foreign policy in the modern world, among both democratic and nondemocratic states, has been to construct what one can call a lighthouse state. Think of a genius in a tower, a great intellectual and a deep student of history—an engaged political practitioner who looks at his country, thinks about its opponents, calculates the national interest, and then with a very clever strategy sets out to trick his enemies and achieve his own goals. Protected from importunate domestic lobbies, the genius in the tower sees farther than the groundlings can; the lighthouse emits the illumination that guides the state. That is the way most people today instinctively think foreign policy "ought" to be made.

This is not just a matter of individual gifted leaders. Very often it requires an institution. In many countries, there are foreign ministries that are largely insulated from domestic political pressures. The mandarins of the foreign office are protected to as large a degree as possible from domestic turmoil as they patiently develop a vision of the national interest and seek to achieve it.

These individuals and institutions often perform well for long periods of time. They do, however, have vulnerabilities. Prince Klemens von Metternich, who dominated the councils of the Austrian Empire for a generation, is rightly renowned as one of the greatest statesmen of European history. But ultimately, his vision of Austria was the product of his background and experience. He was an aristocrat, and the interest of Austria as he saw it was connected to the preservation of the power and wealth of the Hapsburg dynasty and the aristocratic families like his own that surrounded it.

The revolution of 1848 drove Metternich from power and disrupted the delicate balances with which he hoped to maintain Austria's centrality in the world of European power politics. Metternich's skill was extraordinary, but he was only one man—and one particular kind of man. As Austrian society changed under the pressures of economic development and the rise of nationalism, Metternich's methods and aims increasingly diverged from the perceived interests of more and more Hapsburg subjects, and in the end, his policies and power could not be sustained.

That is not the kind of state the American Constitution established. The American state has typically not been a lighthouse state, emitting the radiance that guides the country onto the right path at home and abroad. The founders understood that that kind of centralized state and policymaking was unsuited to the culture of the Americans and the immense range of their interests and concerns. Some other method of deciding among conflicting visions of the national interest would be needed. If the great powers of Europe constructed lighthouses, Americans would build a mirror.

Suppose we think of the national interest less as an abstract concept discoverable by a great intellect and more as the vector of all the local and individual interests held by the various individuals and organizations active in the republic. By developing a political process in which different interest groups are represented in the institutions of government roughly in proportion to their importance in the nation at large, one might arrive at policies that reflect the national interest more accurately than the calculations of the most enlightened genius in the highest possible lighthouse.

This of course is the application in the world of foreign policy of what I've called the Golden Meme, the characteristic idea of Anglo-American civilization that the best order comes from the free play of various elements, each acting in accordance with its own nature. This is Isaac Newton's law of gravity. It is Adam Smith's concept of political economy. It is the theory behind the Madisonian system of checks and balances built into the American Constitution. It is the intellectual basis of Charles Darwin's theory of evolution.

The founders nodded in the direction of the centralized control and coherent planning of foreign policy by giving presidents more power in conducting relations with foreign countries than they had at home. Nevertheless, the Senate's power to confirm nominees for ambassadorships and cabinet posts and the requirement that treaties receive a two-thirds supermajority for ratification ensure that presidents cannot long conduct international relations without the concurrence of Congress.

The traditional or lighthouse system can also be compared to the command structure of a naval ship. The foreign minister or the sovereign is the captain, surveying the seas with a telescope in hand and giving orders to the well-disciplined crew. That is not how the American ship of state works. On the *Good Ship America*, all the sailors are up there wrestling with the captain and one another in a never-ceasing contest to control the ship's wheel.

The result is rarely elegant and often bizarre. American foreign policy wanders erratically and is often unpredictable. Sometimes it seems to head straight for the rocks. But over time, in the long run, one can argue that the American ship's course has corresponded better to the actual interest of the American people than a ship steered by someone with all Metternich's talents but also all his limitations would have done. One of our Founding Fathers, Massachusetts politician Fisher Ames, is reputed to have compared the European model to a man-of-war, sailing gracefully and powerfully until it strikes a reef. A republic, he said, was like a raft. It never sinks, but your feet are always wet.[3]

In opening foreign policy to the interplay of the domestic political order's checks and balances, the founders gave American foreign policy a character that has persisted through many changes of fortune and circumstance. It has not always worked well. Presidents have negotiated complex international agreements, like Woodrow Wilson's Treaty of Versailles and League Covenant and Barack Obama's Joint Comprehensive Plan of Action, only to see domestic opponents frustrate their designs. American foreign policy is sometimes too hot, as in the McCarthyite era of rigid anti-Communism or the post-9/11 frenzy leading to the war in Iraq. It is also sometimes too cold, as with the passive indifference to rising threats abroad that contributed to World War II, the greatest man-made catastrophe in the history of the human race.

No system of governance, however sophisticated and clever, is proof against human folly. The mirror state devised by the founders has, however, enabled the United States to rise over time to become the most prosperous and powerful state that history knows. That is not how state failure looks.

Strategies of Emergence

Mirror states and lighthouse states assess the world in different ways and develop their responses differently as well. A Metternichian lighthouse state is organized around the vision and priorities of a key policymaker, in some cases the highest political authority in the state and in others an official like Metternich himself, to whom, within certain constraints, supreme authority in foreign affairs has been granted. Today, the People's Republic of China is the world's most important lighthouse state. The Marxist-Leninist model of centralized leadership in a one-party state directing the nation's social, economic, and international policies in the service of an overarching ideological vision represents the logical end point of the lighthouse state. Xi Jinping Thought on Socialism with Chinese Characteristics for a New Era, as Xi Jinping's ideas are officially labeled in the Chinese constitution, serves as a source of guidance for all state tasks, including the formation and execution of foreign policy. In a conversation with a Chinese diplomat, I once suggested that Beijing not take published American strategies too seriously, saying that "nobody in any American administration, when confronted by a policy challenge, runs to dust off the office copy of the National Security Strategy to look for guidance on how to respond." My Chinese interlocutor was surprised by this and advised me that that is exactly what Chinese officials do.

There never has been and never will be a foreign policy document for a mirror state that possesses the kind of authority Xi Jinping Thought has in China. Those seeking to understand American national strategy cannot confine themselves to research in official documents and the speeches of senior officials. They must look for patterns in the superficially chaotic path the American raft takes across the stormy seas. Are there general tendencies that become apparent over time, patterns of behavior that continually recur, considerations that over time appear to weigh more heavily on the public mind, and therefore on the policy process, than other, conflicting ideas?

But if the founders' development of a mirror state is one side of their foreign policy, the actual national strategy that gradually took hold during the era of their political activity, culminating in the Monroe Doctrine, was of equal importance.

For the vast majority of American history, the country's foreign policy has been centered on its complex, and often adversarial, relationship with Great Britain and that country's capacity to project power in the Western Hemisphere. Before the Revolution, as part of the British Empire, the American colonies operated within the maritime security system that the British had spent the better part of a century building. Within this framework, the national interests of the American colonies were predominantly commercial and largely aligned with those of Britain. While there were limitations and restrictions designed to give the British a competitive edge—most notably the Navigation Acts—American merchants generally benefited from the protection of the Royal Navy, which allowed them to travel and trade across the world without fear of persecution or piracy. However, business as usual was simply not an option after the end of the Revolutionary War.

While the Revolution had granted the colonies political independence from the British Crown, they remained deeply entangled in and dependent on the British mercantile system.[4] In the three decades leading up to the Revolution, British imports from the American colonies doubled, while British exports—primarily manufactured goods and consumer products—to the colonies tripled. Britain was America's largest trading partner, its largest export market for its staple crops, and its primary source of credit. In the years following the Treaty of Paris in 1783, roughly 90 percent of US imports came from Britain, while nearly a fourth of American exports were bound for Britain.[5] The relationship was asymmetrical, however, as only 6 percent of Britain's imports were from the United States, while the colonies owed British businesses £6 million—more than twice the value of their exports.[6]

Profound disagreements arose over how much the colonies should decouple from Britain after the Revolution, and this very question shaped the first several decades of political debate in Congress; some loathed the thought of partnering with the Crown, while others hoped to learn from the British and, in due time, to emulate them. On one side were the Republicans, led by Jefferson. Wary of British naval power, they favored a stronger partnership with the French, which at the time was the strongest land power in Europe. Without the backing of the French navy and the extension of French finance, the Revolution would have surely ended in defeat. Naturally, Jefferson and others wanted to continue this alliance. Additionally, the French—having recently overthrown their tyrannical monarchy and imposed a new democratic constitution—were, in Jefferson's eyes, not just partners of convenience but ideological brethren.

Many Republicans, including Jefferson, saw trade as an instrument of foreign policy and favored a strategy of aggressive commercial warfare, in part because they believed that it advanced the domestic vision they wished to promote. As Jefferson put it,

> Let our workshops remain in Europe. . . . The loss of transportation of commodities across the Atlantic will be made up in happiness and permanence of government. The mobs of great cities add just so much to the support of pure government, as sores do to the strength of the human body.[7]

Jefferson detested the urbanized, manufacturing-based economies of Britain and Europe that gave birth to a commercial elite who dominated the economy and had an outsized influence on the political process. Fearing that the rise of a similar commercial elite in America would undermine republican virtues and democratic institutions, Republicans viewed this concentration of private wealth—and, as an extension, political power—as a mortal threat to the American experiment in self-government. For Jefferson, societies based on urban modernity and industry—like the European empires—were irredeemably corrupt, prone to venality, runaway speculation, and the degradation of the human spirit. Famously, the Jeffersonians preferred an agrarian-based economy that they believed was better suited to preserving the Republican virtues on which American democracy rested.

In contrast, Hamilton and his allies in Congress and in the Washington administration advocated for a modus vivendi with Great Britain. With the United States separated by more than 3,000 miles of ocean from many of the world's critical global markets, they believed that safe access to maritime routes was a vital national interest. It was the fear of trade disruption, rather than territorial loss, that shaped the Federalists' strategic thinking. For Hamilton and the Federalists, reaching an understanding with the British would alleviate some of these concerns by granting American merchants access to important markets free from persecution or piracy. Moreover, they rightfully recognized that war with Britain would have devastated the young republic's fledgling finances. In 1792, the interest alone on American debt soaked up 87 percent of total revenues, and a massive war would have forced the colonies to take on even more debt while cutting off the primary source of revenue for the federal government—customs duties, which accounted for roughly 90 percent of federal revenue until the War of 1812.[8]

In contrast to Jefferson's disdain for the commercial urbanism in Europe, Hamilton sought to adapt the British system to American conditions. It was his conviction that replicating the British system offered the best chance for the colonies to generate the wealth and power necessary to stabilize America's domestic politics and secure its commercial interests. The British had a powerful executive and the most sophisticated financial markets in the world, which were supported by an independent central bank and a pragmatic, sustainable approach to managing public debt. They also had an integrated national markct, with a strong judicial system that facilitated the rapid exchange of goods and money between creditors and debtors, from India to the Mediterranean to North America. Hamilton believed that the American colonies needed a similarly sophisticated financial system—with deep capital markets and a robust network of creditors and debtors.

A financialized economy would allow the young nation to make the necessary investments in its infrastructure, develop a competitive manufacturing sector, and diversify its economy. As Hamilton argued, this model would grant the colonies

> security from external danger, less frequent interruption of their peace with foreign nations, and, what is more valuable, an exemption from these broils and wars between the parts, if disunited, which their own rivalships, fomented by foreign intrigue . . . would inevitably produce.[9]

From this position, rapid economic growth was a necessary condition for political independence, as it would allow the young republic to amass the resources necessary to check any security threats emanating from across the Atlantic and engage with the Europeans from a position of strength. Additionally, the establishment of integrated national markets and the progression of interstate trade would—so the thinking went—cohere the bickering regional factions into a unified political force. In short, Hamilton believed that realizing this vision would allow the restive colonies to enjoy the sovereignty they had shed so much blood for during the Revolution.[10]

Ultimately, the conflicting visions of the Federalists and Republicans were rooted in divergent views over the relationship between capitalism and democracy, the limits of federal power, and the national interest. This contest nearly broke the United States as the series of revolutionary and Napoleonic wars between England and France consumed Europe and spread across the Atlantic, driving wedges between the pro-British, commercially minded Hamiltonians and the agrarian-based, Francophile Jeffersonians. However, despite some early setbacks, American strategists in both parties would learn to shrewdly exploit the tensions in European politics during this tumultuous period and were able to deliver a series of strategic gains that would ultimately transform this league of states into a continental empire.

Commercial Interests and Federalism

Following the Revolution, the predominant foreign policy issue facing the colonies was essentially commercial: The colonies no longer had unfettered access to international markets spanning from the Far East to the West Indies to the European world and beyond. After the Revolution, the British sought to punish their former colonies by cutting off market access to their possessions in the West Indies, imposing trade restrictions on imports to the British Isles, and arbitrarily levying duties on American goods whenever they saw fit. The elimination of trade with the West Indies was especially ruinous for the New England merchant class, the primary domestic constituency for the Federalists. The New England shipbuilding industry was nearly eradicated, while the once-thriving fishing and whaling industries were devastated. By the mid-1780s, the lucrative cod fisheries off the coast of New England were running at just 20 percent of their prewar level.[11]

While many Americans blamed these difficulties on the evils of British power, in reality, the root of the problem was American weakness stemming from a disorganized and powerless Congress that had no legal authority to control interstate trade, impose duties on imports, or field a respectable military. It showed in the imperial courts of Europe as the bargaining position of American diplomats was undermined time and again. Reflecting on his experience as the French ambassador after the Treaty of Paris in 1783, Jefferson stated that the colonies were "the lowest and most obscure of the diplomatic tribe."[12] With each state assuming the authority to regulate its own commerce, Britain would masterfully play rival states off of one another—exacerbating sectional divisions in the process—as they sought to acquire better trade conditions in American markets while constraining the nation's exports.

Additionally, other European powers enacted a set of trade restrictions aimed at denying American merchants access throughout the Western Hemisphere and across the Atlantic. Spain imposed bounties on American traders along the Mississippi River and at the vital port of New Orleans.

Holland, Portugal, and Sweden slapped heavy duties on American tobacco and rice. France obstructed American shipping to the West Indies and constrained American exports of specific staple crops that directly threatened its own prized monopolies. At every turn, the struggling confederation of states was berated and rejected by its larger European cousins.

Madison, acknowledging the grim commercial realities confronting the United States, remarked, "Our trade . . . entirely contradicted the advantages expected from the Revolution, no new channels being opened with other European nations, and the British channels being narrowed by a refusal of the most natural and valuable one to the US."[13] He assessed that "the trade of this Country is in a deplorable Condition."[14]

The inability of American diplomats to successfully secure the country's trade interests would bring the issue of federal versus state power to the forefront of the national discussion and, as a result, set the stage for the clash between the Hamiltonians and Jeffersonian-led Republicans over the future of the young republic.

The inability of the weak postrevolutionary government established by the Articles of Confederation to protect American commercial and security interests was a major factor leading to the adoption of the Constitution. But while Americans were constructing their new government, the French Revolution was leading Europe into a new series of destructive wars that would test and almost break the new American republic.

Navigating Napoleon

With the outbreak of war between Revolutionary France and Britain in 1793, the United States found itself embroiled in what soon became an intercontinental struggle for global domination between the European empires. Despite this perilous situation for the colonies, the eruption of hostilities between Paris and London provided them with three critical strategic opportunities. First, throughout the course of the revolutionary wars in Europe, the Spanish Empire would suffer a series of defeats in both the Caribbean and Europe that undermined its strategic position in the Western Hemisphere, which opened the door to American westward expansion and, critically, the eventual acquisition of the Louisiana Territory. Second, war dramatically increased demand for American exports, as the maintenance of large standing armies in Europe required increasingly large amounts of raw materials. American sales of cotton, meat, fish, and grains soared as a result, with the total value of American exports increasing from $19 million to $49 million from 1791 to 1807.[15] Third, the titanic military struggle in Europe and into Eurasia would lead to the diversion of military resources and naval assets away from the Western Hemisphere, which helped facilitate the de facto reinstatement of American trade with the West Indies—a formerly vital market for American merchants, particularly those from New England.

Almost immediately following the outbreak of hostilities, there was near-unanimous consensus within government and the halls of Congress that maintaining American neutrality was a strategic imperative. Despite the adoption of the new Constitution, the 13 colonies were still relatively weak and divided. The republic was still struggling to get over the economic depression caused by the Revolution, and the colonies were saddled with enormous debts that made reconstruction nearly impossible. Taxes were even higher than they had been under King George, and real per capita incomes fell by about a third between 1774 and 1790, with the economy contracting by roughly 30 percent between 1774 and 1789.[16] The dark economic conditions exacerbated squabbling in the capital as various regional factions sought funding from an impotent Congress.

To make matters worse, the country was deeply vulnerable to military intervention—or even conquest—by the European empires; Britain still maintained large military contingents around the Great Lakes and in Canada while Spain and France still had sizable footprints in Florida and the Caribbean, respectively. In turn, Congress could not afford to field an army, and the Continental Navy had been disbanded. If the country was going to survive, it desperately needed partners to alleviate its security issues, and it needed injections of capital to remain solvent. However, maintaining neutrality proved to be extremely difficult and deeply polarizing, as American policy vacillated between antagonizing and then pacifying either the British or the French, simultaneously reassuring one and necessarily irritating the other, all while both nations harassed and inhibited American shipping over the ensuing decade.

Within just a few short months after the outbreak of hostilities in 1793, the British, seeking to suffocate the French economy, moved to interdict American merchants trading foodstuff and staple crops with the French. In that time, they seized hundreds of merchant vessels and forcibly conscripted their sailors into the Royal Navy. Enraged by the audacity of their former oppressors, the Jefferson-led Republicans called for retaliatory trade restrictions on the British, while the Hamiltonian-led Federalists, fearing that a commercial war could escalate into open war, pushed for détente.

For the Republicans, America's revolutionary triumph was essentially nullified as long as the colonies remained economically dependent on the British mercantilist system—"Dependence begets subservience and venality," Jefferson lamented.[17] From his perspective, imposing wide-ranging tariffs and aggressively confronting the British would accelerate the process of decoupling, thus granting the colonies the independence they so desperately sought. In contrast, the Federalists viewed aggressive reciprocity as a recipe for disaster, as the financial system that Hamilton sought to build depended on the revenue generated from the relatively free exchange of goods with European powers. The depredation of American shipping, though tragic, was seen as a necessary trade-off for the greater good.

At the behest of Hamilton and the Federalists in Philadelphia, the Washington administration was able to temporarily halt the path toward confrontation with the British following the signing of Jay's Treaty in 1794. Any serious person would acknowledge that Jay's Treaty was a disappointment at best. While it technically granted "most favored nation" status to the American colonies, American diplomats were unable to extract any other major concessions from the British, and critical postrevolutionary issues such as the strategic threat posed by British forces on America's northwestern frontiers as well as the restrictions on American shipping to the West Indies remained unresolved.

Most importantly, American shipping bound for France was still subject to confiscation and American sailors to forcible conscription. For Republicans like Madison and Jefferson, the Jay Treaty was irrefutable evidence that the current state of affairs was untenable: Economic dependence on Britain was incompatible with true political independence. However, at this juncture, avoiding war and appeasing the formidable British Empire was a necessary condition for economic revival.

To make matters worse, the French were furious with the Washington administration and viewed their former allies' new understanding with the British as a treacherous stab in the back. Decrying Charles Pinckney, the American minister to France, French officials proclaimed that they "would not acknowledge nor receive another minister plenipotentiary from the United States," unless the Jay Treaty was dismantled.[18] Soon thereafter, the French seized over 300 merchant ships, driving up insurance rates on merchant shipping and paralyzing Congress. President Adams, desperate to avoid war, was now faced with the seemingly impossible task of somehow smoothing over tensions with the French while avoiding the wrath of the recently appeased British.

Tensions were further inflamed following the infamous XYZ Affair, in which French officials demanded bribes from American diplomats to even begin negotiations. War seemed inevitable. However, due to Adams's steadfast—yet fully necessary—appeasement of Paris, America was able to dodge full-blown war with the French, a war that Adams knew the colonies could not possibly win. Tragically, his conciliatory stance toward Paris made him a one-term president, as many within the Federalist ranks were irate over his refusal to deepen relations with the British and confront the French. As his former allies now turned their back on him in droves, the presidency was handed over to Jefferson and the Republicans in 1800.

By the turn of the century, the American economy's prospects were on a much sounder footing, with substantial economic growth and increased commercial integration into key foreign markets such as the British West Indies. Before the British cut off American trade with the West Indies after the Treaty of Paris in 1783, the region had accounted for nearly a quarter of the future nation's total exports. In turn, the surge in exports provided the colonies with the revenue needed to pay off cumbersome debts left over from the Revolution and turbocharged interstate commerce and urban growth. Critically, the ensuing influx of capital led to the emergence of the monetary and fiscal infrastructure necessary for the issuance of credit, enabling large substantial private investments back into the economy.

The results were astounding. Before the outbreak of war in Europe, the colonies had just three banking institutions, in Boston, New York, and Philadelphia. By 1812, nine of the top 10 companies in the country were banks, and the financial sector comprised nearly 50 percent of the 500 largest corporations across the nation. Moreover, between the outbreak of war in 1793 and the War of 1812, the country saw the rise of a thousand chartered corporations, a figure that dwarfed those of the older European empires.[19] Adams's approach, while conciliatory, undeniably served the national interest, as he needed to ensure that the country could bide its time and make the necessary investments into its economy and military to bolster its long-term strategic position.

Importantly, however, the uneven distribution of economic gains stemming from the revival in trade reinforced political divisions between the Hamiltonian Federalists, who drew support from the commercial centers in New England, and the agrarian-based Jeffersonian Republicans, as the vast majority of these new charters, financial institutions, and commercial enterprises were based in New England and the mid-Atlantic states. Consequently, their opposition to tariffs and commercial warfare was shaped by the fear that not only would such measures halt transatlantic commerce, but their economic contagion would reverse the country's recent fortunes: Banks would likely fail, and new businesses would go bankrupt.

Jefferson, Madison, and the Napoleonic Wars

The Jeffersonian-led Republicans pursued a strategy aimed at economically disentangling America from its former adversary—a strategy that would prove disastrous. As the Napoleonic Wars intensified and the British and French navies continued to pillage American neutral shipping, Jefferson was growing increasingly desperate to avoid being drawn into the European conflict, which had by then escalated into a global war spanning from India to the West Indies. Embracing a trade policy of aggressive reciprocity and heavy tariffs, he passed legislation that essentially shut down US trade with Britain in 1807. The economic implications of Jefferson's embargo were severe: Exports fell by more than 80 percent, from $108 million in 1807 to $22 million in 1808, and imports for domestic consumption dried up by nearly 50 percent. The agrarian, slaveholding South, Jefferson's base of support, was particularly hard-hit, as the prices of cotton, flour, tobacco, and rice declined by 27 percent from December 1807 to June 1808.[20] Eventually, trade tensions would increase with the British and boil over into the War of 1812.

The Americans launched the war in the summer of 1812 when Britain faced a largely united Europe under the leadership of a triumphant Napoleon, with few resources to spare for an American conflict. But Napoleon's reckless invasion of Russia changed the strategic balance, and by the end of the year, Britain had far more flexibility. The ensuing war with Britain would kneecap American trade, with the value of American imports declining from $70 million in 1812 to $13 million in 1813.[21] With just over a dozen battle-ready warships, the American Navy was no match for the larger and more experienced British fleet. By the end of the war, the British had burned Washington, and the American economy was in shambles.

At this time, Britain had defeated Napoleon and the French war machine and controlled a maritime empire spanning from the Strait of Gibraltar to the Cape of Good Hope and the Strait of Malacca. It dominated the fantastically rich Indian subcontinent and had naval bases scattered across the world, from the Mediterranean to the Persian Gulf. Britain boasted close to 45 percent of global shipping, and its fleet had more than 600 warships patrolling the high seas.[22] Fresh off his victories in Europe, the British government offered the Duke of Wellington the command of British forces in the Americas with the objective of ending the upstart republic that had been a thorn in the Crown's side since it had secured its independence.

Still in its restive infancy, the United States came to the realization that it simply couldn't compete with the British Empire and thus sought a modus vivendi with the British Crown. Moreover, by the turn of the 19th century, as the United States began to expand westward, Washington was almost always short on investment, and the country simply didn't have the political capital or resources necessary to underwrite the kind of naval buildup needed to effectively protect its commercial shipping. The result was that the United States sought the agreement with Great Britain that Hamilton and Washington had originally wanted in the 1790s—an agreement that would last until the outbreak of World War I nearly a century later. Under this new understanding, the British would do the heavy lifting abroad, by maintaining a stable balance of power in Europe that would keep any potential threats to American interests bottled up on the Continent. In turn, the United States refrained from directly challenging Britain's international position.

It was British naval muscle, not the American Navy, that enforced the Monroe Doctrine, as the Royal Navy would prevent both the French and the Spanish from reconquering the South American countries that had declared their independence during the Napoleonic Wars. Britain would respect America's commercial interests, refrain from military encroachment in the Western Hemisphere, and, all things considered, leave the youthful colonies to their own devices. Moreover, the triumph of free trade in British politics meant that throughout the 19th century, American access to global markets dramatically increased.[23]

The Raft Reaches Shore

The story of American foreign policy in the generation between the ratification of the Constitution and the proclamation of the Monroe Doctrine
is a story of failed calculations, compromises from weakness, and poor
judgments. Yet the United States emerged from the era of the Napoleonic Wars with significant gains. Territorially, it acquired Louisiana from
Napoleon. Economically, the progress in banking and manufacturing prepared the United States, alone in its hemisphere, to flourish and compete
at the highest levels in the increasingly sophisticated and global economy
that the accelerating Industrial Revolution would promote. Politically,
its ability to survive the storms of European great-power conflict and its
growing size and population made the republic respectable, if not popular, in the courts of Europe. American emissaries would never again meet
the levels of contempt their predecessors endured in the supercilious
18th-century courts.

Behind all this was the reality that America emerged from the founding
era with a strategic orientation. The young republic's commercial interests tied it to the world and, especially, to Europe. And while Great Britain
was America's most serious commercial rival and, potentially, the only
European country with the ability to harm the United States at home,
the mutual Anglo-American interest in a balance of power in Europe, the
importance of British capital for American economic development, and
the promotion of a global economic system provided an adequate basis
for a modus vivendi. That relationship could never be naive; Americans
understood that the British were rivals as well as partners, and Washington would repeatedly have to overcome British opposition as the Americans expanded across the continent.

This strategic accommodation was the dominant reality of not only
American but world history through the remainder of the 19th century.
The relationship continued to shape the 20th century even as the British
Empire fell, and the strategic orientation behind it continues to shape
American calculations even today.

The American presidents of the day had their great moments. Washington's constancy in support of the controversial Jay Treaty, Adams's courageous capitulation to the French, and Jefferson's sacrifice of constitutional principle in the service of securing the Louisiana Purchase are all admirable. But the genius of American foreign policy in those years stemmed more from the efficiency of the constitutional machine at creating a mirror state than from anyone seeking to clamber into a lighthouse. The agricultural interests of the South, the focused attention in the West on the mouth of the Mississippi and the British presence south of the Great Lakes, the commercial interests of New England, and the financial interests in New York and Philadelphia were all affected by the turbulence on the international scene—and their representatives labored tirelessly to get those interests taken seriously in national policy. Presidents and secretaries of state could not dictate; they had to negotiate and compromise.

The strategic orientation that emerged in the early republic has lasted so long, and been so effective, because the structure of the American government permitted the emergence of a foreign policy that reflected the actual interests of the American people in all their variety and diversity. Statecraft matters. Let us hope that the raft of the American republic continues to slosh its way through the currents and storms of many years to come.

Notes

1. The source of this quote is contested, but Nigel Rees offers a helpful discussion of its origins in Nigel Rees, ed., *Brewer's Famous Quotations* (Weidenfeld & Nicolson, 2006), 306.

2. Enoch Powell, *Joseph Chamberlain* (Thames & Hudson, 1977), 151.

3. Ralph Waldo Emerson attributed this line to Ames in his 1844 essay "Politics." Available in Ralph Waldo Emerson, *Essays: First and Second Series*, ed. Irwin Edman (Harper Colophon Books, 1981), 412.

4. A. G. Hopkins, *American Empire: A Global History* (Princeton University Press, 2018), 110, 180.

5. Douglas A. Irwin, *Clashing over Commerce: A History of US Trade Policy* (University of Chicago Press, 2017), 96.

6. Walter Russell Mead, *Special Providence: American Foreign Policy and How It Changed the World* (Routledge, 2002), 113.

7. Thomas Jefferson, *Notes on the State of Virginia*, ed. William Peden (University of North Carolina Press, 1954), 77.

8. These figures draw on the historical tables made available by the Office of Management and Budget at White House, "Historical Tables," https://www.whitehouse.gov/omb/information-resources/budget/historical-tables/.

9. This quote is from Hamilton's original draft of Washington's Farewell Address. It can be found in *Selected Writings and Speeches of Alexander Hamilton*, ed. Morton J. Frisch (AEI Press, 1985), 436.

10. Alexander Hamilton, "Alexander Hamilton's Final Version of the Report on the Subject of Manufactures," December 5, 1791, Founders Online, https://founders.archives.gov/documents/Hamilton/01-10-02-0001-0007.

11. Gordon C. Bjork, "The Weaning of the American Economy: Independence, Market Changes, and Economic Development," *The Journal of Economic History* 24, no. 4 (1964): 541–60, https://www.jstor.org/stable/2115760.

12. Quoted in Bradford Perkins, *The Cambridge History of American Foreign Relations*, vol. 1, *The Creation of a Republican Empire, 1776–1865* (Cambridge University Press, 1993), 56.

13. Perkins, *The Cambridge History of American Foreign Relations*, 1:56.

14. James Madison to Richard Henry Lee, July 7, 1785, Founders Online, https://founders.archives.gov/documents/Madison/01-08-02-0168.

15. Douglass North, "The United States Balance of Payments, 1790–1860," in *Trends in the American Economy in the Nineteenth Century* (Princeton University Press, 1960), 581.

16. North, "The United States Balance of Payments, 1790–1860," 588.

17. Jefferson, *Notes on the State of Virginia*, 71.

18. Charles Cotesworth Pinckney, *Dictionary of American Biography*, ed. Dumas Malone (Scribner's, 1934), 615.

19. Richard Sylla and Robert E. Wright, "Scale and Scope in Early American Business History: The 'Fortune 500' of 1812," Working Paper No. 224 (Institute for New Economic Thinking, August 3, 2024), https://www.ineteconomics.org/research/research-papers/scale-and-scope-in-early-american-business-history-the-fortune-500-of-1812.

20. Douglas A. Irwin, "The Welfare Cost of Autarky: Evidence from the Jeffersonian Trade Embargo, 1807–1809," Working Paper No. 8692 (National Bureau of Economic Research, December 2001), https://www.nber.org/papers/w8692.

21. North, "The United States Balance of Payments, 1790–1860," 583.

22. Hopkins, *American Empire*, 84.

23. Walter Russell Mead, *God and Gold: Britain, America, and the Making of the Modern World* (Alfred A. Knopf, 2007), 160.

About the Authors

Lindsay M. Chervinsky is the executive director of the George Washington Presidential Library and a historian of the presidency and American political culture and institutions. She is the author of *The Cabinet: George Washington and the Creation of an American Institution* (2020).

Eliga H. Gould is a professor of history at the University of New Hampshire and the author of *Among the Powers of the Earth: The American Revolution and the Making of a New World Empire* (2012).

William Anthony Hay is the associate director for public programs and professor in the School of Civic and Economic Thought and Leadership at Arizona State University and the author of *The Whig Revival, 1808–1830* (2004).

Walter Russell Mead is the Ravenel B. Curry III Distinguished Fellow in Strategy and Statesmanship at Hudson Institute, the Alexander Hamilton Professor of Strategy and Statecraft at the Hamilton Center for Classical and Civic Education at the University of Florida, and the "Global View" columnist at *The Wall Street Journal*. He is the author of *Special Providence: American Foreign Policy and How It Changed the World* (2001).

Jeremy Rabkin is a professor emeritus of law at the Antonin Scalia Law School at George Mason University. He is the author of *Law Without Nations? Why Constitutional Government Requires Sovereign States* (2005).

Gary J. Schmitt is a senior fellow in the Social, Cultural, and Constitutional Studies department at the American Enterprise Institute.

About the Editors

Yuval Levin is the director of Social, Cultural, and Constitutional Studies at the American Enterprise Institute, where he also holds the Beth and Ravenel Curry Chair in Public Policy. The founder and editor of *National Affairs*, he is also a senior editor at *The New Atlantis*, a contributing editor at *National Review*, and a contributing opinion writer at *The New York Times*.

Adam J. White is the Laurence H. Silberman Chair in Constitutional Governance and a senior fellow at the American Enterprise Institute, where he focuses on the Supreme Court and the administrative state. Concurrently, he codirects the Antonin Scalia Law School's C. Boyden Gray Center for the Study of the Administrative State.

John Yoo is a nonresident senior fellow at the American Enterprise Institute; the Emanuel S. Heller Professor of Law at the University of California, Berkeley; and a senior research fellow at the Civitas Institute at the University of Texas at Austin.

The American Enterprise Institute for Public Policy Research

AEI is a nonpartisan, nonprofit research and educational organization. The work of our scholars and staff advances ideas rooted in our commitment to expanding individual liberty, increasing opportunity, and strengthening freedom.

The Institute engages in research; publishes books, papers, studies, and short-form commentary; and conducts seminars and conferences. AEI's research activities are carried out under four major departments: Domestic Policy Studies, Economic Policy Studies, Foreign and Defense Policy Studies, and Social, Cultural, and Constitutional Studies. The resident scholars and fellows listed in these pages are part of a network that also includes nonresident scholars at top universities.

The views expressed in AEI publications are those of the authors; AEI does not take institutional positions on any issues.

www.ingramcontent.com/pod-product-compliance
Lightning Source LLC
Chambersburg PA
CBHW020201090426
42734CB00008B/897